Hello William...

(It's Me, Dad).

Dwayne Taylor

ISBN: 978-0-578-88509-4

Published by Dwayne Taylor

Hello William,

Hello William, my name is Dwayne Taylor, and YOU are my son. I am writing my thoughts to you because I cannot tell them to you personally. The reason I cannot talk to you is because your mother won't allow it. What is the reason for this? Son, I honestly don't know. This is a question you need to ask your mother. You will probably read this same quote a few times. Many things have happened in the past between her and me, resulting in us not being together. But only she can tell you her side of this story. Why doesn't she want me around you? Why does she want to raise you without me? Does she prefer another man raise you? Once again only she can explain this to you.

My primary goal is for these words to find you, so that I might explain my side of the story to you. I cannot express to you how frustrating and painful it is to not be with you. I have been denied bonding with you, looking in your eyes, feeling you squeeze my fingers, touching your hair, hearing your first words, watching you take your first steps, watching you sleep, seeing you smile while you sleep, exploring the world and watching you become this little person. I don't want you to ever go through life thinking I don't love or care about you. I am in love with you, son! I don't want you thinking I gave up on you. I have not! I have tried repeatedly to see you. I contact your mother weekly, attempting to see you. I will continue to try to see you until the day God takes me. So, until the day I see you or God takes me home, here is where I will tell you about myself and the family I feel are important for you to know. I will tell you the story about your mother and me, and my efforts to be with you. I will also attempt to help you avoid my mistakes and teach you a few lessons to get you through life. Lessons and rules a father should teach his son.

My secondary goal is to be one of the voices for the fathers in this world who are doing all they can to take care of their children but cannot because of the many obstacles they encounter, including an unjust justice system and bitterness resulting from bad relationships. There is a popular stigma in the country that men are always the deadbeats or that they don't want to take care of their children. Honestly, son, there are some men in this world who want nothing to do with their children. But there is also a great number of men who want to be in their children's lives. I want to be in your life son, and I want you in mine.

My final goal is to encourage those men out here who are not taking care of their children. I can't honestly understand why they don't because children are awesome! Our children need us! You have a big brother and raising him is beyond awesome! He is 6 years old right now and he asks about you almost daily. He's a great kid, but more about him later.

I pray this book finds you, William! I am not sure what age you will be when or if that happens. I'm using very simple words so you can understand what I mean, if you should find it at a young age. However, some of my subject matters and language should only be exposed to you when you are older and more mature. The reason for this is because you are not always going to be a child. You are going to grow to be a man. I need to do my part the best way I can. There are so many things I need to convey to you and the best way to start is from the beginning.

I am Dwayne Rashawn Taylor. I was born on June 23, 1977, to Wayne Taylor and Blythe Johnson. At that time, I lived on Monticello Ave with my mom, grandmother, and aunt. My father lived on Atlantic St.; both in Jersey City, New Jersey. They were both just teenagers when they had me. Your grandmother and grandfather were only 16 years old. As you can probably imagine, it was pretty difficult for them to have a child so young. But they never gave up! They persevered. You will learn here and in your studies, our people have persevered through a lot in this country. That drive, relentlessness, and perseverance is inside of you. I will talk about your grandparents and our people in greater detail later on.

Growing up in the late 70's early 80's in Jersey City for me was great. I grew up in a time before cell phones, cable networks, and the internet. I grew up at a time when it was a luxury to have a television or telephone in the house. In my house, we had one rotary phone and one small black and white television. Look up rotary phones when you get a chance, so you can learn about our struggles, kid! I spent every second I could outside. Back then, it was much safer than it is today to be outside at a young age alone with your friends. We lived on the second floor in our apartment building. My mom would simply open the window and scream my name to check on me. And I better be there, and I better respond! If I didn't, when I got in the house, she would lecture me about it. You will learn as you get older a lecture from your mom is the worst! If I wasn't outside or playing with my few toys, I was in front of that small television. Especially on Friday night and Saturday morning! I could not miss the Muppets or Knight Rider on Friday and I certainly could not miss my Saturday morning cartoons.

I have lived in a number of places in Jersey City. I spent most of my childhood and life, in ward "F". This section of the city is referred to as "Jackson Hill", more popularly "The Hill". There are even more sections within "The Hill", like "Bergen-Lafayette" and the "Junction" to name a couple. Just a quick history lesson, the neighborhood was named after Thomas and John Vreeland Jackson. They were brothers who were able to buy property in Jersey City and freed slaves. During the civil war, their property became safe houses for the Underground Railroad. The Underground Railroad is a very popular part of our history with the face of it being Harriet Tubman. I'm sure your mother will talk about her one day. Your mother loves strong women. I lived in another part of the city known as the heights, that's like the northern part of Jersey City. It's also known as Hudson City or Sparrow Hill. There is so much history within our city, I recommend you research it, son.

I attended grammar school at St. Patrick's in Jersey City. While in grammar school, I met some of the best people ever! To this day, I am still close to a few of them. I, then, attended Marist High School in Bayonne, NJ. When I was in high school all I wanted to do was play football. I wish I played more sports though in hindsight. From there I attended Hudson County Community. There I obtained a degree in Culinary Arts. I have mixed feelings about school. Some of the curriculum taught is trash. How about they teach you how to stay out of debt, how to save money, how to start a business or a trade, how to grow your own food, and human rights? I would rather learn about that than Hamlet. It is ingrained in this country that you must go to college in order to make it in this world. Son, the truth is you can go to college and still not make it. I am not sitting here telling you not to go to college. What I'm trying to say is always have a plan B and C. I encourage you to find a trade like plumbing, construction, electricity, etc....always have something you can fall back on.

I have only had a few jobs in my life. My first real job was a store clerk in a supermarket. I was still in high school at the time in 1995. This was probably the job where I had the most fun. I met some great people here as well. People I still have in my life. I worked hard there, but I think I had more fun than I worked. This was one of my first steps in adulthood. Making your own money is one of the best feelings in the world, son. Being independent and not having to depend on your parents or anyone is one of the best places you can be in life. I also met my first adult girlfriend. While I held that job, I became a chef at a family owned catering hall. That was a tough job because you work very long hours on your feet all day in a hot kitchen. The best thing I learned from that place is to never go into business with your family! At this point, I got yet another job. In 2000, I became a janitor for the housing authority of Newark. The reason I got the third job, was because your big sister was on the way! Son, this was the worst job I ever had! I absolutely hated it! My direct boss was an idiot and some of the people there were not nice. I wanted to quit this job everyday! But I couldn't because I needed more money to take care of your sister. There are two lessons I want to teach you here. One, before you decide to have children, marry the woman of your dreams and make sure you have the job or career you want first. Two, do not keep a job that you hate! It will stress you out so much that it will affect other areas of your life. Do not put yourself in a position where you live check to check and you have to keep this dreadful job. Please learn from my mistakes.

In 2003, I got my dream job. I became a firefighter in Jersey City. Since I was 4 years old, I have wanted to become a firefighter. I wanted to become a firefighter because my father was one. It is 2019, as I am writing this, and I am still a firefighter. I love it today just as I loved it the first day I walked into the firehouse. Son, find a job you love, if you do that, it will never seem like work. It is extremely fulfilling. I would tell you to think about becoming a firefighter. Your great grandfather, grandfather, and I have done it. So I know it's in your blood. However, your mother would strongly oppose to it. She never liked the idea that I was one.

I like to think of myself as a cool, laid-back person. I try to be thoughtful, considerate, and kind. I am a bit of a goofball. I enjoy smiling and being happy. I am a morning person. I love sports, especially football. The New York Giants is "our" favorite football team. I love food!

Especially BBQ ribs and every sweet known to man! I love being around family. I like going out but I'm primarily a homebody. I love vacationing though. If you share any of these similarities you got it naturally.

I love television…my favorites are cop shows like "Law and Order" or "Criminal Minds". I recently find myself enjoying serial killer shows. I don't empathize with any of the killers, if you were wondering, I just find it fascinating how some people think. I love all types of music. I can listen to rap and the next song could be soft rock. My favorite artists currently are Eminem, Lizzo, Notorious BIG, Michael Jackson, Prince, Elton John, The Beatles, etc. This list goes on and on. I like talented musicians. If your taste in music is all over the place, you got that naturally, too. The only illness I suffer from at this time is high cholesterol. Bad eyes run in the family also, most of us wear glasses. Hopefully, your eyes will be better, and you won't need glasses.

That's pretty much it about me. I'm pretty simple.

FAMILY

Now I'm going to tell you how I feel about family and tell you about our family. I feel everyone lives a certain way, which is to say everyone lives their lives according to certain morals or values learned at home. Beginning here, I'm going to share with you my morals and values. Every true father wants their children to grow up better than he did, most want their child to grow up with their beliefs.

- Always take care of your family.
- Don't let a funeral be the only reason you come together with family.
- Make sure you reach out on special occasions. Ex: Christmas, Birthdays etc.
- Always try to attend events the family invites you to.
- Accept your family for who they are. Never judge them.
- If you have it, give the kiddies some money.
- Always respect the elders, especially the women in the family.
- When the elders in the family speak to you, listen.
- Never stand by, while a family member is struggling.

I have been blessed with great families on both sides. In our family, we have beautiful people that were and are good, hard-working people. Our family consists of doctors, nurses, firefighters, teachers, and the list goes on and on. We have family that loves to be together and support one another. There are so many people in this world that have no one. Though this world has millions of people in it, there are many who have no one. I deeply desire to expose you to our family so you will never feel you are alone in this world. There are times when you are going to feel your parents won't understand you. This is when it's good to have an aunt, uncle, or a cousin to talk to. On this side of the family, you currently have your father, two grandparents, a sister, a brother, aunts, uncles and a few cousins. Unfortunately, you have no great grandparents, about whom I will be telling you first.

Great Grandfathers

Your great grandfather on my mother's side was a soldier in the air force. He became a family man and had 5 children. He was a Jersey City resident all his life. He loved a family get together and he was a good cook too. He would have cookouts as often as he could. I remember going to his house for cookouts, it was an all-day affair. Every food you could imagine was on the menu; ribs, steak, burgers hotdogs, even potatoes and corn. Christmas was a huge thing in his house. The early part of the day was dedicated to gift opening, while the latter was the big Christmas feast. His wife was a great baker so there were multiple cakes, pies, and other pastries. Those were very good days. His wife is still alive today. However, he passed away in 2016 due to sepsis.

Your great grandfather on my dad's side was a trailblazer. He was a soldier in the army and fought in World War II. He was the first Black firefighter in Jersey City back in 1950. He was a co-founder of an organization within the Jersey City Fire Dept named the Vulcan Pioneers. This organization (of which I am currently the president), basically tries to help out the less fortunate in the community of Jersey City. He was also once the President of the NAACP which is the National Association for the Advancement of Colored People. The NAACP fights for equality for black people and against discrimination. Many things that he accomplished were to help someone else. He took the blows, he took the hatred, he was the punching bag so people like you and me could get ahead in life. He was a great man and good grandfather to me. According to my mother he was the one that helped her get home from the hospital after I was born. He was good to me. He would always slip me a few dollars when I was young. He would buy me cakes and snacks from the store. There would always be a box of brownies or cupcakes in the house when I visited. He had a stroke in the mid 80's and passed away in the early 2000's. He lived in Jersey City the majority of his life then was taken to North Carolina to live out the rest of his life. I don't know if strokes run in the family, but make sure you always take care of yourself, son.

Great Grandmothers

Your great grandmother on my mom's side was one of the best women I have ever met in my life. As I mentioned before, I lived with her, my aunt, and my mom at a young age. She was the family leader, and she did the job well! When there was a problem in the house, grandma handled it, no matter how big or small. If someone tried to break in the house, grandma handled it. If there was a math problem I couldn't solve, grandma handled it. She kept the roof over our heads, food on the table, and the house clean. She would work hard at her job everyday then come home to fix us a hot meal. She wore many hats...she was the chef, the toy repairman, the plumber, the teacher, the security guard, the house doctor, the referee, the coach and more. She was one of the best cooks ever! She offered food to anyone that entered her house. She accepted every family member for who they were no matter what they did in the past. People need this type of forgiveness, son. You never know what a person has gone through. No one can choose their upbringing or who raises them. Everyone is going to struggle with something in life. The least we can do as family members is not judge and instead help them. She held a few jobs, including a beautician, an office worker, a teacher's aid, etc. She was a very hard worker. We never missed a meal. She sacrificed so much for us. It was the norm for her to put us first. She was tough. Before she passed away, she suffered from high blood pressure, hypertension, gout; and she was a cancer survivor. She passed away in 2016 of dementia.

Your grandmother on my dad's side was another beautiful, strong woman. She was a nurse and had 3 children. She was a goofball and always made me laugh. What was so special about her, to me, was how serious she was when she took her wedding vows. The part that asks, "Will you love your husband in sickness and health?" As I mentioned, my grandfather suffered a stroke and she stood by him until his last breath. She worked extremely hard taking care of him! I remember helping her at times, realizing how difficult it really was. It was no different than taking care of a baby. The only difference was that my grandfather was over 200 pounds and he was never going to recover, he was only going to get worse. She dedicated her life to taking care of him. I deeply admired her for her sacrifice and love for her husband. Her passing was a shock as well and painful to me. I was planning on visiting her in North Carolina not realizing how sick she truly was. I didn't make it there because I let life get in the way, which is why I am telling you, don't push off visiting family, son. Take some time to visit loved ones.

Losing my grandparents was an excruciatingly hard pill to swallow. To be very honest it crushed me. I can't find too many things in this world more painful than losing a family member. I tried to prepare myself for their passing. I knew one day it was going happen. When it eventually did, I wasn't ready. My father has a saying, "Time don't heal nuttin!" He is right! You just have to learn how to accept it and get on with life. We all take loss of life differently. As a man, you have to understand while you are mourning, you may have to be someone else's strength. This can be a difficult thing at times. But you have to do it!

Your Grandfather (My Father)

Your grandfather was born in Jersey City, NJ August 7, 1960. As I mentioned before, he was the youngest of three. He was a street kid but a hard worker. His first job was as a paperboy at 10 years old, I believe. As long as I can remember he always had a job. He was a store clerk, an exterminator, a security guard, a car washer, a dispatcher, and more. He played a few sports, but his favorite was football. He played football all the way up through college. He didn't finish college, back then, because he had an opportunity to become a firefighter. He was a great firefighter! You have to see his medals display case one day! There are so many war stories people tell me about him. Like the day he caught a lady that jumped out of a top floor window of a two-story building It is because of my father that I wanted to be a firefighter. I have always admired my father's work ethic and passion for the job. It is because of him I am who I am today. I honestly don't know what I would be doing with my life right now if it wasn't for my dad. I know I would be successful, but I wouldn't be as happy as I am today at any other job. When I was 10 years old, my mom and dad separated. I didn't see my dad as much as I would have liked to. He was always there if I needed him, but it wasn't the same as it was before with him just popping up to see us or take us out to dinner. My father went on to get married and he had 5 more children. He had 4 with his wife and 1 with another woman while married. Yes he had an affair. Yes, papa was a rolling stone! He was a good man, but he wasn't perfect. He always took care of his family. He always made sure we had a place to stay, food on the table, and clothes on our backs. There were times he struggled but he still made things work. Protecting and providing for the family is the man's primary responsibility.

Your Grandmother (My Mom)

Your grandmother was born in Jersey City, NJ; May 1, 1961. She was the oldest of 2 (on her mother's side). She was the big sister and, having a hard-working mother, she found herself babysitting often and taking care of the house at a young age. She was a smart girl but shy. She was skipped a grade in school which is how she met my father. She had me when she was 16 years old. Back in the 70's, this was not a common thing. So as you can imagine life at times was difficult. Not only was it physically demanding, but it was emotionally draining to listen to people's opinion of her. She was a child herself trying to raise a baby and barely able to get a job. She was a black teenager with a baby living in the "ghetto". People told her she was going to be a failure. She went on to finish high school, then she attended Saint Peter's College on a full scholarship. After college, she went on to become an accountant. She decided at a later time in life to change careers, so she went back to school and became a nurse. She is currently a nurse and back in school again. Throughout my life, my mother has been my everything! As I mentioned before, my father married and began a family with his wife. My mother moved out of her mother's house shortly after. She took care of everything we needed. I never went without a place to sleep, clothes on my back, or food in my stomach. There were too many times to count when she put my wants and needs before her own. I remember she'd save up every penny she had so we could have a good Christmas. I honestly can't remember a time where I felt afraid or nervous because I knew my mom would take care of us. I could always talk to her about anything. It didn't matter how big or small the problem she would never judge me, and she answered the question honestly. I didn't approach her with life-changing issues all the time, but at times I needed advice. She provided the same attention and honesty to my friends. There have been many times my friends sat down and talked to my mother. She remains to be a very special person in my life. Without her, I wouldn't be here. I am not the only person upset about not being able to see you. Your grandmother is upset as well. I have been fortunate enough to spend some time with you. She has never been able to see you or hold you. It is exceedingly difficult to understand why you are not with us. My mother is very family oriented. Family is significantly important to her. You not being included or involved in our lives is not fair to her or you. She isn't going to give up hope of one day seeing you. She is a wonderful grandmother. She wants

20

you here with us. She wants you to know that your family loves you and needs you here.

Your Sister

Your sister was born on September 13, 2000 in Bayonne, NJ. I was in love with her the first moment I laid eyes on her. I instantly felt the need to better myself so I could take care of her. I didn't hesitate to find a better job, that is when I got the job in Newark. Being with her while she grew up has been one of the best experiences of my life. She is the one that made me a dad. She made me grow up. She was a great baby and little girl. Today, she remains to be a sweet woman. She is currently in college trying to finish there and enter medical school. She looks forward to meeting you. She would make a great big sister for you because she already is a big sister!

Your Brother

Your brother was born on February 14, 2013 in Princeton NJ. He's said by many to be a love baby because he was born on Valentine's Day. He truly is. He is one of the sweetest guys I know. He picks a flower on his way back from school for his mother. If he knew you liked something and saw it in the store he would ask me to buy it for you. He reminds me a lot of my grandmother. I hesitated in telling him that you were born because I knew he would want to see you. I was right! Every time I leave the house to go to Jersey City he asks if I am going to see you. There was a short period of time I was allowed to see you by order of the court. He wanted to come with me a few times to see you, and it broke my heart that I couldn't take him. The court wouldn't allow it. Though he hasn't met you, he speaks of you often. He wants to meet you. He would make a great big brother for you!

24

Your Aunts

You have 9 aunts. Yes nine! To break it down, you have 5 aunts who are my sisters and 4 aunts who were sisters of your grandparents. I can't speak of all of them individually, though they are worthy, it would simply take up too much time. They range from nurses to sales reps to homemakers and more. Some took care of me and some have taken care of my children. Your absence has not sat well with any of them. You are a part of our family and they all look forward to meeting you as well.

28

Your Uncles

I don't have any brothers, so your uncles are the brothers of your grandparents. We have 3 uncles. One is a college professor that had his own speech therapy business. Another is a computer consultant. The last is a businessman who works for a mortgage company. I'm closer to the professor. He has been a constant and positive role model in my life. When my dad married and moved on, at times, I felt alone. My uncle was there for me to look up to. Don't get me wrong, when I called for him, my dad was there. But as a young kid it didn't always feel that way. That feeling is something I don't want you or any of my children to feel. I always want to be there for you! This same uncle had a fight with cancer that he won! He is the only family member on that side of the family that I know had cancer, so you know.

William, you need to know who you are and where you come from. I want to expose you to these wonderful people. Our family is full of good, loving people. They would love to have you around. One of them could be the one who influences you and makes you take a certain path in life. Your uncle's career choice may interest you and you may become a college professor, or your sister may inspire you to become a doctor. I simply want to expose you to all the great things and people I have been exposed to.

Your Cousins

33

YOUR MOTHER

I'm going to share with you the story of your mother and me. This section is going to include a ton of text messages between her and me, emails, and court documents involving you. In the text messages your mother is (W Cell).

I met your mother online in 1998. That was the new thing at that time. We talked on the phone here and there for a couple of years. A few times we talked on the phone all night. I remember getting on the phone with her at 10 in the evening and talking until the sun began to rise. We had very deep conversations about our futures and things we liked, sometimes we had heated debates about nothing. It was all in good fun. I would win some of the debates though she would deny it. I knew I won because I left her speechless. I used to think, 'Wow she's very smart.' She always had some knowledge about what we talked about, which later on became almost anything. Later in life, I learned that she knew so much because she knew she was going to start a debate with me that night, so she prepared herself by researching whatever the topic was going to be! Either it was the water shortage in the world, or which is better Coke or Pepsi. At that moment, I formed an attraction to your mom that was different for me. It wasn't a physical or sexual attraction, it was a mental attraction. I enjoyed talking to her. What attracted me the most was her drive and determination. She knew what she wanted in life. She wanted to be a lawyer, and she accomplished that later on. She would wake up at 4 in the morning to finish homework while in high school. Everything she did, she

34

did it 100%. Because of this attraction, I had to meet her. I attempted to meet her on two separate occasions, and both times she stood me up. We later spoke on the phone and she revealed that both times she was nervous about meeting me. This was frustrating but my attraction to her wouldn't go away. I voiced my frustrations to her and gave her an ultimatum. I told her I was going to try to meet with her one last time and, if she didn't come out, I wasn't going to try again. She finally came out to see me and we went to Starbucks on Pavonia Ave. I thought your mom was beautiful and had the prettiest smile. Talking to her over a cup of hot cocoa was just like our all-night conversations. It was perfect! We talked so long the employees had to tell us to leave because the store was going to close. We talked a little while longer and I eventually took her home, which was only around the corner. I knew at that time I had to see her again. I wasn't in love, but I was highly attracted to her. We did meet again, and we went out to eat at a restaurant on Grand Street, which at that time was called the Grand Bank. Dinner was just like our first meeting. The conversation was nice and deep. From there we talked more and spent more time together and the attraction grew.

As I mentioned, I only had a mental attraction with your mother in the beginning, so I was dating another woman. Your sister was born around this time and I tried to form a connection with her mother, but she didn't seem to want that. Honestly, I didn't know what your sister's mother really wanted. She seemed to want me around but was more focused on school and, with a baby around, it didn't make our relationship any easier. I wasn't able to talk to her and be around her like I had in the past. This made me feel neglected and lonely, which led me to talk to your mother more causing more of an attraction. At this point, we still weren't dating, but we talked more frequently. Eventually, we did start dating. Dating your mom at the beginning was amazing. We had a lot of wonderful times together, but we did bump heads a few times. Your mother wanted to be in a serious relationship, I did as well but I declined. The reason was because I had a young child and I wanted to always put her first. I didn't want a relationship to interfere with raising your sister. I also didn't want your mother involved in my drama or decision-making concerning your sister. This frustrated your mother deeply, as a result she got involved in another relationship. The only problem I had with her getting into another relationship was that she didn't tell me!

While your mother was mentally and emotionally leaving me, I was trying to pull her in. Though I had made some questionable decisions, in my heart and mind I wanted to be with your mother. I fully understood her desire to move on, I just didn't understand the way she went about it. She still acted as if she and I were in a relationship. She never told me she had entered into a new relationship. It crushed me to discover the truth. I have had my heart broken in the past, but it was nothing like that time. I had finally learned what Lenny Williams and Bonnie Raitt were singing about. I was absolutely sick to my stomach, I even lost weight. I was depressed and I felt alone. I said all that to tell you despite all that heartbreak, I made it through! Son, in your lifetime someone may break your heart, or you will lose a loved one. It's going to feel like someone ripped your heart out of your chest. I'm here to tell you, you will make it past that! It may seem impossible at the time, but I promise you if you just pray, ask God to help you, calm down, take deep breaths, talk to friends and take it one day at a time you will make it on the other side of that pain. I'm going to be honest, you may never get over it, but you will learn how to deal with it. It took some time, but I got over your mom (or so I thought) and moved on with my life.

I moved on and reconciled with your sister's mother and we had your brother. While I was happy in that relationship and it was going well, it had its issues. Perhaps the problems before weren't addressed properly or I wasn't over your mother. To be honest, it was both. If problems aren't addressed, they cannot be corrected. As far as the relationship with your mom, she seemed to have just left without an explanation. There was never any closure, so that left more questions than answers. As time went on, we occasionally spoke here and there on holidays and birthdays. We are both passionate and emotional people, so we did talk about some of the issues we had with each other in the past. There was some closure. We would speak every day and then sometimes not for months.

As quickly as your mom disappeared from my life, she reappeared. It was like the cycle was starting over again. She entered my life again almost the same way she entered it before. Things started off the same way, slow at first. But this time we were both in relationships. So we attempted to be friends. I still had deep feelings for your mother, so the platonic friendship did not last long. As I mentioned before we were both in relationships. My relationship was good, but it had some issues I felt I couldn't deal with, leaving me in a very stressful position. I was with a woman with two children and I shared a house with her. She was a good person, I loved her; and the relationship was good, but I wasn't happy. Bottom line was I wasn't over your mother. I wanted to give us another chance. So, I decided to leave the relationship I was in. It wasn't as simple as just leaving. Remember we had two children and a house. So, I had a conversation with my current girlfriend, and we split up. Only problem was I was still living in the house. To make this already complicated situation even more complicated your mother confessed to me that she wasn't only in a relationship, but she was in fact married. According to your mother she didn't enjoy being married. After a very short time, he became very neglectful and abusive.

Hearing and reading all this in her messages gave me mixed emotions. I was angry that she was going through this at home. Hearing the fear build up in her voice when it was close to the time he got home from work made me feel so bad for her. I told her to leave and just move back in with her mother. I constantly asked her why she stayed. She told me she stayed because she was married. She made this confession on my birthday. I was shocked and hurt because I had asked her in the past if she was married and she told me she was not. Don't get me wrong, I'm not innocent in this and I'm no one to judge, but I wasn't married! We had been away on trips, we spent the night together many times and we had been intimate, all while she was married! Call it stupidity or being head over heels in love, despite everything, I still wanted to be with her.

Your mother and I decided to wait to get into a serious relationship because of all the issues. We wanted to enter our new relationship with a clean slate. I would move out of my house and she would get divorced. We had even started looking at areas to purchase a house and had conversations about starting a family. The plan was to get together in the summer of 2018.

At this time, all was going well. The thought of living with your mother was making me happy and we spoke of it often. She had gone on a trip to Mexico with her mom and while there, she experienced some sickness. She didn't think much of it, she figured it was the food she was eating. However, when she returned home the sickness continued. She decided to take a pregnancy test and the results of that test were positive. She was pregnant with you.

9/2/17, 4:37 PM - W Cell: would you be upset if im pregnant?

9/2/17, 4:38 PM - Dwayne Taylor: Not at all

9/2/17, 5:28 PM - Dwayne Taylor: Think u would make a good mom

9/2/17, 5:28 PM - W Cell: i already know u are a good dad

9/2/17, 5:29 PM - W Cell: oh boy. we sure love to do things the complicated way

We had a plan for the following summer to be a couple and start trying to have children. But at times, emotions got the better of us and we talked about having children sooner. You are probably thinking we are both crazy by now. Being in love with a person makes you do crazy things, son. Emotions have no logic. We were planning a vacation for November. On this trip we were going to start trying to have children. Little did we know your mother was already pregnant with you.

8/26/17, 6:54 PM - Dwayne Taylor: Ok... U wanna stop taking pill for our vacation ?.. And see what happens?

8/26/17, 6:55 PM - W Cell: yes

8/26/17, 6:55 PM - Dwayne Taylor: U sure?

8/26/17, 6:55 PM - Dwayne Taylor: U gotta stop taking it a month before

8/26/17, 6:56 PM - W Cell: im sure. are u sure?

8/26/17, 6:57 PM - Dwayne Taylor: Yes.. Bring it

8/26/17, 6:57 PM - W Cell: lol ok.

We both had suspicions that she might be pregnant. She had morning sickness, she had missed her cycle, and she got strange symptoms like not wanting to eat meat. Sure we talked about trying on our next vacation, but that was emotion talking. Reality was setting in and, as previously mentioned, this relationship was complicated enough. We talked about options, if she was pregnant.

9/3/17, 9:06 PM - Dwayne Taylor: If u are... What do u want to do?

9/3/17, 10:20 PM - W Cell: didn't u say it wasn't ideal?

9/3/17, 10:20 PM - Dwayne Taylor: I did... But not if its already here

9/3/17, 10:21 PM - W Cell: so it made it seemed like u wouldn't want to

9/3/17, 10:21 PM - W Cell: I wouldn't want to put u in a bad situation

9/3/17, 10:21 PM - Dwayne Taylor: Noooo

9/3/17, 10:22 PM - W Cell: ok

9/3/17, 10:22 PM - Dwayne Taylor: I feel u don't control situations like this

9/3/17, 10:23 PM - Dwayne Taylor: If ur pregnant than we ready!

9/3/17, 10:23 PM - W Cell: what u mean?

9/3/17, 10:23 PM - Dwayne Taylor: Gotta be

9/3/17, 10:23 PM - W Cell: ok

9/3/17, 10:23 PM - W Cell: ok

9/3/17, 10:23 PM - Dwayne Taylor: I want u to keep it if u r

Your mom has issues dealing with stressful situations. When she was going through things with her husband she visited a psychiatrist.

10/2/17, 8:52 AM - W Cell: my anxiety level is so high!

10/2/17, 8:56 AM - Dwayne Taylor: Make a list of important stuff

10/2/17, 9:02 AM - W Cell: I know but you know I have abnormal levels of anxiety

10/2/17, 9:02 AM - W Cell: nothing pains me more than to hurt someone else....hence the reason I stayed with him so long

10/2/17, 9:23 AM - W Cell: do u think his conduct towards me was abusive m

10/2/17, 9:23 AM - W Cell: ?

10/2/17, 9:26 AM - Dwayne Taylor: Yes!

10/2/17, 9:26 AM - Dwayne Taylor: I said so... A doctor has said so

She needed help with her anxiety and depression. So, what was going on now definitely had her anxiety level high. She was already going through so much. Despite all that, I made it clear if she was pregnant I wanted to keep the child.

On September 9, 2017, your mother purchased a pregnancy test form the store. The days prior to that, she was still feeling sick and her mother had her doing things like lifting heavy boxes. It wasn't her fault really, she had no idea what was going on. I kept pestering her to take the test so we could end all the suspense, but your mother wanted to take it with me present. We finally got together that evening and she took the test. The test came back positive. She was pregnant with you!

I wasn't surprised at the result and neither was she. I had so many emotions running through my mind. I was happy, excited, confused, and worried; all at the same time. I was happy and excited because I wanted to share a child with your mom, and I thought it was what we both wanted. I was confused because I thought she and I had a plan to start a family the following summer. I thought, 'Why would she stop taking her birth control after we came to an agreement, and with everything going on?' I was worried because I didn't know how she was going to explain all this to her soon to be ex-husband and her mother. What was she really going through and how was she feeling mentally? Your mom went through so many emotional ups and downs. Here she was jobless, preparing for a divorce and now pregnant. She was able to get a job, so that took a little weight off her shoulders. I felt bad about everything she was going through but frustrated at the same time because she wouldn't talk to me or listen to any of my suggestions.

9/11/17, 2:02 PM - W Cell: hi. i have been thinking about my start date and dates needed off. I am going to tell them September 27th. They told me that November is their busiest month of the year. November will also probably be around the time I will tell them about the pregnancy. I am wondering if u are willing to be creative with me as far as vacation. would you be open to doing a long weekend, and a local retreat for the rest of the time. We can rent a nice place maybe even in New Brunswick, go to the spa, nice dinners. I know it isn't ideal but I just don't want to give up the $ and I want to make a good impression given I'm gonna be asking for a lot a time off. I am not sure what my medical situation is going to be. I would totally understand u wanting to do something else.

She eventually told her employer, and everything worked out okay on that end. Sharing this news with her husband and mother and getting things in order still lingered though. I didn't want to add any more stress, but I had to ask why she stopped taking her pills.

9/12/17, 10:48 PM - W Cell: yes, i did mess up with my pills during July but i didn't stop taking them altogether

As I just mentioned, I didn't want to add stress. So I left it alone, but in most cases a person would have to stop taking pills for almost a month to get pregnant. You were planned. Just not at that time. I always told your mom as much as we try to have control of our lives we are not in control. God is in control. She and I didn't plan for you at that time, but God did, and I accepted it. She told her mother she was pregnant the next day.

9/13/17, 5:39 PM – W Cell: i told her

9/13/17, 5:39 PM - Dwayne Taylor: And?

9/13/17, 5:39 PM - W Cell: it was how I thought

9/13/17, 5:39 PM - W Cell: it was ok

9/13/17, 5:39 PM - W Cell: I made bad decisions blah blah blah

9/13/17, 5:40 PM - W Cell: get a divorce

9/13/17, 5:40 PM - W Cell: im gonna look bad

9/13/17, 5:40 PM - W Cell: stuff like that

I knew your grandmother wasn't going to take it well, but I wanted her to be a little happy for her. But that wasn't the case. She was worried for your mom and that was fully understandable. The news wasn't received well, but at least her mother now knew and we could move forward. We continued sharing houses we had seen online and talking about living together in the future.

9/16/17, 10:52 AM - Dwayne Taylor: Looking at nice houses

9/16/17, 10:52 AM - W Cell: ohh ok

9/16/17, 10:53 AM - W Cell: nice

9/16/17, 10:53 AM - Dwayne Taylor: I think we can afford a 600 000

9/16/17, 11:18 AM - W Cell: I think so

9/16/17, 11:40 AM - Dwayne Taylor: I sent u some houses

9/16/17, 11:40 AM - Dwayne Taylor: No in law suites though

9/16/17, 11:40 AM - Dwayne Taylor: Is ur mom down with retiring or Gettin a job elsewhere?

9/16/17, 12:45 PM - W Cell: sent them via email?

9/16/17, 12:45 PM - W Cell: I think she wants to retire

9/16/17, 2:40 PM - W Cell: we should look into a custom house...see what we can get in our range

We even spoke about your big sister moving in with us.

9/21/17, 1:20 PM - Dwayne Taylor: Told rec she may have to move in with u n i

9/21/17, 1:21 PM - W Cell: and what did she say?

9/21/17, 1:21 PM - Dwayne Taylor: U know

9/21/17, 1:22 PM - W Cell: ok

9/21/17, 1:22 PM - Dwayne Taylor: Yup

We talked about you often. I knew you were going to be a boy. I often referred to you as "he or 'him'" in conversations. We had many conversations about you and, of course, we debated about everything as usual.

10/1/17, 10:52 PM - W Cell: but with a child...things will be tight. it will be ok though

10/1/17, 10:52 PM - W Cell: glad it makes u smile

10/1/17, 10:53 PM - Dwayne Taylor: Not as much as u think

10/1/17, 10:53 PM - Dwayne Taylor: Ur gonna be tired...

10/1/17, 10:53 PM - Dwayne Taylor: More than u will be broke

10/1/17, 10:53 PM - W Cell: we shall see lol

10/1/17, 10:54 PM - Dwayne Taylor: Most u spending on a baby is 50 bucks a month

10/1/17, 10:54 PM - Dwayne Taylor: On average

10/1/17, 10:54 PM - W Cell: overall budget increases

10/1/17, 10:55 PM - W Cell: $50? we will see

10/1/17, 10:55 PM - Dwayne Taylor: Not really.. U n I didn't have a budget

10/1/17, 10:56 PM - W Cell: ok

10/1/17, 10:56 PM - Dwayne Taylor: Yes baby... Unless u find a way to spend extra money

10/1/17, 10:56 PM - Dwayne Taylor: I'm assuming we don't need childcare

10/1/17, 10:57 PM - W Cell: yeah

My mom was also excited you were coming. From the first moment she met your mother, she instantly liked her; actually she adored her. When she knew your mom was coming over to the house, she would go shopping so she could make a nice dinner and her famous Piña Coladas. They were very close; and they would hang out without me. They used to go to Broadway shows together, the movies, and dinner dates all without my knowledge. When she found out you were coming along, she immediately wanted to plan a baby shower. My mother wanted your mom and me to get married before your arrival. She didn't know your mom was already married. I didn't want to end her excitement at that time by telling her.

9/24/17, 7:41 PM - W Cell: i called your mom back

9/24/17, 8:50 PM - W Cell: she wants us to get married before the baby comes lol

9/24/17, 8:51 PM - W Cell: i was like....we'll think about it lol

9/24/17, 8:51 PM - Dwayne Taylor: Yea... I don't see that happening. She doesn't know

9/24/17, 8:51 PM - W Cell: i know

9/24/17, 8:51 PM - W Cell: but i could be divorced by then...maybe

9/24/17, 8:52 PM - Dwayne Taylor: You ain't

9/24/17, 8:52 PM - W Cell: i have to be!

9/24/17, 8:52 PM - W Cell: my goal is no later than jan or feb

My mom wanted to plan the baby shower.

9/24/17, 9:26 PM - W Cell: and she wants to be "involved " and plan showers and all that. she is soooo excited. i think more than u and i

Your mom and I figured we would share everything at the right time. We both had other family and friends to tell. We thought we would handle the most important things first, which was monitoring her health and continuing to look for a place to live. While that was going on though, things started to get a little strange. Conversations started to go in a different direction. Your mom started approaching things like she was going to be on her own. She started making budgets using just her income and basically driving herself crazy. I spent most of the time trying to keep her calm.

10/14/17, 6:19 PM - W Cell: having a child us expensive

10/14/17, 6:20 PM - W Cell: is

10/14/17, 6:33 PM - Dwayne Taylor: Nah

10/14/17, 6:34 PM - Dwayne Taylor: Depends on what u think need

10/14/17, 6:43 PM - W Cell: i can't rely on your calculations lol....u always underestimate

10/14/17, 6:43 PM - W Cell: i was just calculating the basics....for next year and it total several thousand

10/14/17, 6:45 PM - W Cell: im gonna be poor lol

50

10/14/17, 6:46 PM - Dwayne Taylor: My goodness....

10/14/17, 6:46 PM - Dwayne Taylor: Put down the calculator

10/14/17, 6:46 PM - Dwayne Taylor: Ummmm... U know ingot two kids right?

10/14/17, 6:47 PM - W Cell: I am sorry but I need to budget for next year

10/14/17, 6:47 PM - Dwayne Taylor: And it ain't cost no 1000s

10/14/17, 6:47 PM - W Cell: but u guestimate

10/14/17, 6:47 PM - Dwayne Taylor: Baby

10/14/17, 6:47 PM - W Cell: u don't factor in everything

10/14/17, 6:47 PM - Dwayne Taylor: What are u calculating?

10/14/17, 6:47 PM - Dwayne Taylor: I think u factor in too much

10/14/17, 6:48 PM - Dwayne Taylor: U need food..clothes..diapers and wipes... Regularly

10/14/17, 6:48 PM - Dwayne Taylor: That's really about it

10/14/17, 6:48 PM - Dwayne Taylor: And u don't nerd clothes that much

10/14/17, 6:50 PM - W Cell: just getting the car seat, stroller, sleeper and breast pump is easily 1500

10/14/17, 6:50 PM - W Cell: not to mention my medical

10/14/17, 6:50 PM - W Cell: and the baby's medical

10/14/17, 6:51 PM - Dwayne Taylor: The hell are u buying!?

10/14/17, 6:52 PM - Dwayne Taylor: Listen... Ill buy that

10/14/17, 6:52 PM - Dwayne Taylor: Baby... It ain't gonna cost that much

10/14/17, 6:52 PM - Dwayne Taylor: We ain't Gettin no expensive stroller.. Cause we barely gonna use it

10/14/17, 6:53 PM - W Cell: yes it will over the cost of the year

10/14/17, 6:53 PM - W Cell: and i will be using the stroller

10/14/17, 6:53 PM - W Cell: a breast pump alone is 400

10/14/17, 6:53 PM - Dwayne Taylor: What U using stroller for?

10/14/17, 6:53 PM - W Cell: to walk around

10/14/17, 6:54 PM - W Cell: i dont live in the suburbs yet lol

10/14/17, 6:55 PM - Dwayne Taylor: But u will... And u aint gonna have the baby in the cold

10/14/17, 6:55 PM - Dwayne Taylor: And not to mention... Baby U ain't gonna be alone

10/14/17, 6:55 PM - W Cell: that is why u need a nice one

10/14/17, 6:55 PM - Dwayne Taylor: I promise... Long as I'm living it ain't gonna cost that much

10/14/17, 6:55 PM - W Cell: but anyway, everything adds up

10/14/17, 6:56 PM - W Cell: im not trying to be cheap

10/14/17, 6:56 PM - W Cell: it costs what it costs

10/14/17, 6:56 PM - Dwayne Taylor: U ain't trying to save either!

10/14/17, 6:56 PM - W Cell: of course I will try to save

10/14/17, 6:57 PM - Dwayne Taylor: And u gonna have a shower... I bet most of that is a gift

10/14/17, 6:57 PM - W Cell: but when u add up everything for next year it will be in the thousands, even if u are being cheap

10/14/17, 6:57 PM - W Cell: my mom tried to talk me into that today when i was pricing things out

10/14/17, 6:58 PM - W Cell: i just don't want to deal with it...u can have one lol

10/14/17, 7:01 PM - Dwayne Taylor: Babe... Everything cost 1000s

10/14/17, 7:02 PM - Dwayne Taylor: I promise a baby might cost 100 a month... Not including big things

10/14/17, 7:02 PM - Dwayne Taylor: Relax... We will be aight

10/14/17, 7:05 PM - W Cell: please...life insurance and college savings (hopefully i can start) is more than that. diapers, clothes, added transportation, child care services when needed, food, gear from diaper bags to bouncy seats, medical co pays, furniture for room, misc, nice clothes

10/14/17, 7:08 PM - W Cell: u have had an unique situation, especially with tyce...

10/14/17, 7:19 PM - Dwayne Taylor: Look

10/14/17, 7:19 PM - Dwayne Taylor: None of that is deeply important

10/14/17, 7:19 PM - Dwayne Taylor: Insurance is like 25 dollars a month

10/14/17, 7:19 PM - Dwayne Taylor: Not impossible

10/14/17, 7:19 PM - Dwayne Taylor: Nice clothes... Not important

10/14/17, 7:20 PM - Dwayne Taylor: U will see

10/14/17, 7:20 PM - Dwayne Taylor: Only thing that's important and a must have right now is food and diapers!

10/14/17, 7:32 PM - W Cell: im sorry but i disagree. medical insurance for child cost money every month, insurance even if it is 25 a month that is quarter of your 100 budget lol. im not having a kid in poverty, im just gonna be cash poor

10/14/17, 7:33 PM - W Cell: bath tub thingy, toiletries, and the baby will need stuff period

10/14/17, 7:34 PM - W Cell: im not gonna carry around diapers in a shoprite bag lol

10/14/17, 7:34 PM - W Cell: i am trying to develop a realistic budget for next year

10/14/17, 7:34 PM - W Cell: if u don't want to help with that, that is fine

10/14/17, 7:34 PM - Dwayne Taylor: Babe... My kid is covered

10/14/17, 7:35 PM - W Cell: it isn't free!

10/14/17, 7:35 PM - Dwayne Taylor: It is for u n baby

10/14/17, 7:35 PM - W Cell: we will see

10/14/17, 7:35 PM - Dwayne Taylor: We need on diaper bag baby...not 1 a month!

10/14/17, 7:35 PM - Dwayne Taylor: One

10/14/17, 7:35 PM - W Cell: i know but im getting a budget together for next year

10/14/17, 7:36 PM - Dwayne Taylor: Just stop

10/14/17, 7:36 PM - W Cell: some things will be one time purchases

10/14/17, 7:36 PM - Dwayne Taylor: Just enjoy now baby...please

10/14/17, 7:36 PM - W Cell: enjoy? doesn't mean not planning

10/14/17, 7:36 PM - Dwayne Taylor: Ok.. Figure 250 a month...is that far?

10/14/17, 7:43 PM - W Cell: oh boy

10/14/17, 7:47 PM - W Cell: and btw, what exactly am I supposed to be enjoying right now? lol

10/14/17, 7:52 PM - Dwayne Taylor: Becoming a great mom

10/14/17, 7:52 PM - Dwayne Taylor: U gonna be a mom!!

10/14/17, 7:52 PM - Dwayne Taylor: Geez

10/14/17, 7:52 PM - Dwayne Taylor: Stop making everything a business

10/14/17, 7:52 PM - Dwayne Taylor: Enjoy...dag

10/14/17, 7:53 PM - Dwayne Taylor: Think about reading stories...

10/14/17, 7:53 PM - Dwayne Taylor: And them darting in they sleep

10/14/17, 7:53 PM - Dwayne Taylor: Farting

10/14/17, 7:53 PM - Dwayne Taylor: And putting on wigs

10/14/17, 7:54 PM - Dwayne Taylor: And board games...(that U let them win Whitney)

10/14/17, 7:54 PM - Dwayne Taylor: And snowball fights

10/14/17, 8:23 PM - W Cell: that is just not my personality lol

10/14/17, 8:23 PM - W Cell: i have got a lot serious things to think about it

10/14/17, 8:24 PM - W Cell: it isn't all unicorns and rainbows

10/14/17, 8:24 PM - Dwayne Taylor: Do u ever think of nice fun things?

10/14/17, 8:24 PM - Dwayne Taylor: And it ain't tacks and nails either baby

10/14/17, 8:24 PM - Dwayne Taylor: I think of finances... But it don't consume me

10/14/17, 8:25 PM - W Cell: it is important to me. money isn't gonna fall from the sky

10/14/17, 8:25 PM - W Cell: im thinking about getting a part time job

10/14/17, 8:26 PM - W Cell: something easy

10/14/17, 8:28 PM - W Cell: anyway, things for me to think about

10/14/17, 8:28 PM - W Cell: how is your evening?

10/14/17, 8:34 PM - Dwayne Taylor: No... Baby it is important

10/14/17, 8:34 PM - Dwayne Taylor: It is!

10/14/17, 8:34 PM - Dwayne Taylor: But lets see what we got first... I think we will be ok.

10/14/17, 8:34 PM - Dwayne Taylor: Let the situation dictate second jobs

10/14/17, 8:35 PM - Dwayne Taylor: U are barely home now.. A second job would keep u out the house even longer

10/14/17, 8:35 PM - Dwayne Taylor: And take away family time... Which I think is deeply important

10/14/17, 8:56 PM - Dwayne Taylor: Ur mom didn't have much when having u...in fact she was poor

10/14/17, 8:57 PM - Dwayne Taylor: Am I correct?

10/14/17, 9:24 PM - W Cell: yeah but who wants that situation?

10/14/17, 9:27 PM - Dwayne Taylor: No just making a point we are better off than both our parents

I knew so many emotional, mental, and physical things were going on with your mom. I tried my best to listen and comfort her. Every single day we communicated, she was concerned or stressed out about something. I just wanted her to relax and take a breath. I repeatedly told her I would be there, and I would help her the best way I could. I told her the only thing that would stop me from trying to take care of her is if she pushed me away. But nothing I said seemed to bring her any comfort. It was frustrating to keep reassuring her and trying to convince her I would be there, only for her to ignore it and carry on with the same questions and concerns. I already had 2 children, I wasn't new to the game. I knew what we needed and what had to be done. Your brother and sister were well taken care of and still are to this day!

It was a seesaw of emotions. One day she's telling me she loves me and wants nothing more than to spend time with me, asking how she could be better in our relationship, then the next day she's telling me she wants to be alone.

11/11/17, 7:12 AM - W Cell: hi

11/11/17, 7:12 AM - Dwayne Taylor: Good morning baby

11/11/17, 7:20 AM - W Cell: ive been up for a while

11/11/17, 7:20 AM - W Cell: miss me?

11/11/17, 7:22 AM - Dwayne Taylor: U know I do sweet stuff

11/11/17, 7:23 AM - W Cell: u love me?

11/11/17, 7:23 AM - Dwayne Taylor: Deeply

11/11/17, 7:23 AM - W Cell: love u

11/11/17, 7:24 AM - Dwayne Taylor: U my baby

11/11/17, 7:24 AM - W Cell: that's right

11/11/17, 7:25 AM - W Cell: my mom is talking a mile a minute this morning

11/11/17, 7:26 AM - W Cell: what would you like more of from me?

11/11/17, 7:26 AM - Dwayne Taylor: Lol

11/11/17, 7:27 AM - Dwayne Taylor: Sex

11/11/17, 7:27 AM - Dwayne Taylor: Ur attention

11/11/17, 7:41 AM - W Cell: how could I give you more attention?

11/11/17, 7:41 AM - Dwayne Taylor: Wanting to be around me

11/11/17, 7:41 AM - W Cell: more time? texting?

11/11/17, 7:41 AM - Dwayne Taylor: More time with me

11/11/17, 8:25 AM - W Cell: u should know that i always want to be around u

11/12/17, 3:54 PM - W Cell: I know u feel like we haven't been spending much time together. And, even though I have been sick a lot, which has prevented me from doing manu things, overal I just have found it easier to deal with things emotionally from a physical distance.

11/12/17, 3:55 PM - Dwayne Taylor: Ok. In Just hope its a temporary thing

11/12/17, 3:55 PM - Dwayne Taylor: I wanna be close to U. Mentally and emotionally

11/12/17, 3:56 PM - Dwayne Taylor: I don't want distance from u

11/12/17, 9:14 PM - W Cell: I know this is going to sound crazy but I'm going to start looking for another job...not aggressively. But if I see something, I will send my resume in

11/12/17, 9:37 PM - Dwayne Taylor: Y. I thought u liked it?

11/12/17, 9:41 PM - W Cell: it's fine. but maybe i can find a job that i like and pays more

11/12/17, 9:41 PM - W Cell: i wouldn't leave for less or the same

11/12/17, 9:42 PM - Dwayne Taylor: What ever u think is best babe

11/12/17, 9:42 PM - W Cell: making more $ is best

11/12/17, 9:43 PM - W Cell: financially, i just don't see this working

11/12/17, 9:43 PM - W Cell: long term

11/12/17, 9:43 PM - Dwayne Taylor: We can rent

11/12/17, 9:43 PM - W Cell: even still

11/12/17, 9:44 PM - Dwayne Taylor: Ok

11/12/17, 9:44 PM - W Cell: I just need to make more

11/12/17, 9:48 PM - W Cell: In order for me to feel comfortable, I need to be be to live financially independent not codependent. I need to be to support myself and do better than barely making it. 75k is like making min wage in NJ

11/12/17, 9:52 PM - Dwayne Taylor: But baby... The plan was U do this I. Order to start ur own thing

11/12/17, 9:52 PM - Dwayne Taylor: In not i

11/12/17, 9:54 PM - W Cell: yeah im not changing the plan

11/12/17, 9:54 PM - Dwayne Taylor: But more money means more work

11/12/17, 9:54 PM - W Cell: maybe not

11/12/17, 9:54 PM - Dwayne Taylor: U looking in ny?

11/12/17, 9:55 PM - W Cell: but I need more money...i have to get my head out of the clouds

11/12/17, 9:55 PM - W Cell: no

11/12/17, 9:55 PM - Dwayne Taylor: Do u get a raise in a yr?

11/12/17, 9:55 PM - W Cell: a raise isn't gonna make a difference

11/12/17, 9:56 PM - W Cell: not a sizeable one

11/12/17, 9:57 PM - Dwayne Taylor: Well do what works for u

11/12/17, 9:57 PM - W Cell: A job making more money works better for everyone, i think

11/12/17, 9:58 PM - Dwayne Taylor: Yes

11/12/17, 9:58 PM - Dwayne Taylor: Just want u to be happy

11/12/17, 9:58 PM - Dwayne Taylor: Do what u feel u need to

11/12/17, 9:59 PM - Dwayne Taylor: It what's the most u think you can make at place u are now?

11/12/17, 9:59 PM - W Cell: I don't know exactly

11/12/17, 10:00 PM - Dwayne Taylor: A guess

11/12/17, 10:00 PM - W Cell: I don't know

11/12/17, 10:00 PM - Dwayne Taylor: There was no scale

11/12/17, 10:00 PM - W Cell: it isn't a government job

11/12/17, 10:00 PM - W Cell: only government jobs provide scales

11/12/17, 10:01 PM - Dwayne Taylor: Ok

11/12/17, 10:01 PM - Dwayne Taylor: Would u give this job a chance to match?

11/12/17, 10:02 PM - W Cell: nah

11/12/17, 10:02 PM - Dwayne Taylor: Ok

11/12/17, 10:02 PM - W Cell: that doesn't usually work out

11/12/17, 10:03 PM - W Cell: that is usually viewed as being disloyal and that person is more likely to be fired down the road

11/12/17, 10:04 PM - W Cell: it will be hard for me to find a position right now...but I will look

11/12/17, 10:05 PM - Dwayne Taylor: Ok

11/12/17, 10:06 PM - W Cell: This job is serving it's purpose for now. So I am grateful but I can't just become complacent

11/12/17, 10:07 PM - Dwayne Taylor: Its not complacent when u have a chance to grow... And u happy

11/12/17, 10:07 PM - W Cell: this job can't support me, and I felt better admitting that to myself this weekend

11/12/17, 10:08 PM - Dwayne Taylor: Ok

11/12/17, 10:08 PM - W Cell: It's okay

11/12/17, 10:08 PM - Dwayne Taylor: Do what's gonna make u happy baby

11/12/17, 10:08 PM - Dwayne Taylor: And let u live or do what u want

11/12/17, 10:10 PM - W Cell: Right now, I am moving into survival mode. Being happy with a job is important but part of thar is compensation

11/12/17, 10:11 PM - Dwayne Taylor: Ok

11/12/17, 10:11 PM - Dwayne Taylor: Don't get in ur own way

11/12/17, 10:11 PM - W Cell: I no longer have the luxury of doing what makes me happy. I am snapping out of that mindset...

11/12/17, 10:11 PM - W Cell: im not

11/12/17, 10:12 PM - Dwayne Taylor: Yes u can do what makes u happy... U just sometimes gotta stop to go to work

11/12/17, 10:12 PM - W Cell: I have to make enough

11/12/17, 10:12 PM - W Cell: and right now im not

11/12/17, 10:13 PM - Dwayne Taylor: U r right... For where u r

11/12/17, 10:13 PM - W Cell: i crunched the numbers a lot of ways, it is not going to work

11/12/17, 10:13 PM - Dwayne Taylor: U r right now I meant

11/12/17, 10:14 PM - Dwayne Taylor: Its not gonna work for house "A"

11/12/17, 10:14 PM - Dwayne Taylor: I don't want u over working urself

11/12/17, 10:14 PM - Dwayne Taylor: U need to have time for home

11/12/17, 10:15 PM - W Cell: Home is important

11/12/17, 10:17 PM - Dwayne Taylor: Ok

11/12/17, 10:17 PM - W Cell: when i said 75k was my bare min...that was last year

11/12/17, 10:18 PM - W Cell: before a child

11/12/17, 10:18 PM - W Cell: now things are much different

11/12/17, 10:18 PM - Dwayne Taylor: I understand.

11/12/17, 10:19 PM - W Cell: so I have to make adjustments where I can

11/12/17, 10:20 PM - W Cell: but anyway, didn't mean to go on that tangent

11/12/17, 10:21 PM - W Cell: just wanted to say I will start looking again

11/12/17, 10:21 PM - Dwayne Taylor: Aight

I understood wanting to make your own money and being independent, even though I told her I was going to be there. I later learned that her going into "survival mode" wasn't limited to finding a more suitable job. It also meant she was getting into a mindset where she was going to be taking care of you without me. To this day, I don't know why she went in this direction. I know women go through a lot of hormonal changes when pregnant, but how did she get there?

On November 18, 2017, your mom had a doctor's appointment. I took her to the appointment, and we discovered there was a complication with you. She was told to immediately go to the hospital. While there, we found out you were basically trying to be born. Guess you couldn't wait to be in the world. I can't really get into the specific details but basically your mother's body couldn't hold you in. She had a surgery, and your mother was told to stay in bed for the rest of the pregnancy. Your mother was around 4 months pregnant at this time.

11/20/17, 4:47 PM - Dwayne Taylor: U talk to people at work?

11/20/17, 7:25 PM - W Cell: told them about being in the hospital and that i had surgery but no details

11/20/17, 8:13 PM - Dwayne Taylor: I gotta tell them

11/20/17, 8:16 PM - Dwayne Taylor: U

11/20/17, 8:22 PM - W Cell: yea, I'll figure it out

11/20/17, 8:23 PM - Dwayne Taylor: Just tell.. But u gotta ask can u work from home.. Or do something

11/20/17, 8:24 PM - W Cell: Yeah, I will let them know what they need to at this point. I don't know the future of this pregnancy so no need to disclose too much

11/20/17, 8:25 PM - Dwayne Taylor: Do u think something is going on with baby?

11/20/17, 8:27 PM - W Cell: I don't know if I want to or should go forward, there is a lot of risk and I have to been sure I can handle it, especially if there is a pre-term birth

11/20/17, 8:31 PM - Dwayne Taylor: Is that what the doc said?

11/20/17, 8:33 PM - W Cell: it is what i am saying

11/20/17, 8:34 PM - W Cell: he said it is a risk either way

11/20/17, 8:34 PM - Dwayne Taylor: Yes

11/20/17, 8:34 PM - Dwayne Taylor: Not high

11/20/17, 8:35 PM - W Cell: this is a high risk pregnancy

11/20/17, 8:35 PM - Dwayne Taylor: Ok

11/20/17, 8:35 PM - W Cell: I have a lot to think about this week

11/21/17, 2:17 PM - Dwayne Taylor: Hope u do take it easy

11/21/17, 3:30 PM - W Cell: yeah, i am. I go to doctor next tuesday

11/21/17, 3:32 PM - Dwayne Taylor: Ok

11/21/17, 3:33 PM - Dwayne Taylor: Would u like me to take u?

11/21/17, 3:35 PM - W Cell: Don't worry about it. I should be able to drive by then, plus I am not sure how long it will be. Might be a couple hours or more for the appointment. I can't promise a certain end time.

11/21/17, 3:36 PM - Dwayne Taylor: Ok

11/21/17, 3:36 PM - W Cell: but after the appointment, I should have a better idea of next steps

11/21/17, 3:36 PM - Dwayne Taylor: Ok

11/21/17, 3:51 PM - Dwayne Taylor: Doc said it was ok to drive?

11/21/17, 3:55 PM - W Cell: well I'm going back to work Monday either way so I am going to have to drive. A week from driving has to be enough.

11/21/17, 3:56 PM - Dwayne Taylor: Babe.... Yo... Doc said no work

11/21/17, 4:01 PM - Dwayne Taylor: You're going to hurt yourself

11/21/17, 4:21 PM - Dwayne Taylor: Hello?

11/21/17, 7:01 PM - W Cell: I am not working this week, keeping things light. Just ran out to get rx filled.

11/21/17, 7:01 PM - W Cell: day slowing down?

11/21/17, 7:02 PM - Dwayne Taylor: But babe the doctor said no work

11/21/17, 7:03 PM - W Cell: well i don't have to luxury of not working indefintely

11/21/17, 7:07 PM - Dwayne Taylor: Its not indefintely

11/21/17, 7:08 PM - Dwayne Taylor: Its 5 months

11/21/17, 7:08 PM - Dwayne Taylor: Its not good for U or the baby

11/21/17, 7:08 PM - Dwayne Taylor: Can u see if u can work from home?

11/21/17, 7:09 PM - Dwayne Taylor: U was gonna look for a new job ne way

11/21/17, 7:17 PM - Dwayne Taylor: Can u ask the doctor again

11/21/17, 8:11 PM - W Cell: I have to call him tomorrow anyway because I had a little issue today. I will ask

11/21/17, 8:15 PM - Dwayne Taylor: Ok

11/21/17, 8:16 PM - W Cell: i might have done a little too much this evening but at least i seeing what the limits are

11/21/17, 8:16 PM - Dwayne Taylor: Why

11/21/17, 8:16 PM - W Cell: i am

11/21/17, 8:16 PM - Dwayne Taylor: U gotta chill

11/21/17, 8:16 PM - W Cell: I had to go to the drug store

11/21/17, 8:16 PM - Dwayne Taylor: Why arent u listening?

74

11/21/17, 8:16 PM - Dwayne Taylor: U don't want this

11/21/17, 8:17 PM - W Cell: I needed my prescription

11/21/17, 8:17 PM - Dwayne Taylor: The doctor said u don't leave the house!

11/21/17, 8:18 PM - W Cell: I needed my prescription!

11/21/17, 8:18 PM - W Cell: I need that too!

11/21/17, 8:18 PM - W Cell: otherwise a miscarriage can happen

11/21/17, 8:19 PM - Dwayne Taylor: When I asked did u need something why didn't u say that?... I was downtown

11/21/17, 8:19 PM - Dwayne Taylor: This morning

11/21/17, 8:20 PM - W Cell: how was I supposed to know u were in the area?

11/21/17, 8:21 PM - W Cell: but anyway, it was taken care of

11/21/17, 8:34 PM - Dwayne Taylor: I really dont know what's important to u

We have been here before. She was, again, setting the pieces to leave the relationship and blaming me for it instead of just being honest and saying she wanted to end it. That pretty much set the tone for the rest of our relationship.

This caused tension between your mom and me, we barely communicated. The only communication was when I would reach out to make sure she was okay, attempting some conversation but we mostly argued. I also saw her twice to try to smooth things out, but it didn't work. Your mom and I never really argued in person. If we did have words, I always tried to approach the next encounter with that argument behind us. I don't like drama and I never try to keep it going. Arguments are necessary in relationships and, at times, good. They show where both people stand and help get issues discussed. But if arguments continue then other measures need to be taken. I guess your mom's approach was to let the relationship dissolve. I deeply loved your mom and tried all I could to make the relationship work. She simply didn't feel the way I felt.

12/28/17, 7:16 AM - W Cell: Good morning

As stated previously, I didn't mention anything for money. That was just an example. I have work this morning and other stuff going on. So please hold on to your money. Thank you.

12/28/17, 7:47 AM - Dwayne Taylor: I know u didn't mention it for money. But u never gave me the total. We had conversations about it that U was suppose to get back to me about and u didn't. The money is sitting in the bank. Ill give it to u Friday or when ever

12/28/17, 7:48 AM - Dwayne Taylor: But nah I'm giving u money... So I don't gotta hear about me not keeping my word anymore

12/28/17, 7:49 AM - Dwayne Taylor: After I give u money u can't use that argument anymore. So I wanna give that to U most urgently!

12/28/17, 7:49 AM - Dwayne Taylor: I'm forgetful. I didn't mean to not give u ur money. That's not me

12/29/17, 7:57 AM - Dwayne Taylor: Morning u want me to drop off money today?

12/29/17, 10:08 AM - Dwayne Taylor: Ok.. Hope your well today. Have a good day

12/30/17, 8:42 AM - Dwayne Taylor: Good morning!!! Would you like me to drop off that money today?

12/30/17, 10:12 AM - Dwayne Taylor: Well... I've tried 3 days already... Hope u well. Have a good day

12/31/17, 7:35 AM - Dwayne Taylor: I can not come today.   Happy New Year. Hope you are well. I can bring you the money tomm

1/1/18, 1:28 PM - Dwayne Taylor: Well Happy New Year to U.

1/1/18, 1:29 PM - Dwayne Taylor: Hope u have a good year

1/1/18, 1:43 PM - W Cell: Thanks and Happy New Year to you and your family

1/2/18, 7:48 AM - Dwayne Taylor: Good morning

1/2/18, 10:30 AM - W Cell: Good morning

1/2/18, 10:30 AM - Dwayne Taylor: How r u?

1/2/18, 10:30 AM - W Cell: I'm ok. And you?

1/2/18, 10:33 AM - Dwayne Taylor: I'm good thanks

1/2/18, 10:33 AM - Dwayne Taylor: Just checking on u

1/2/18, 10:43 AM - W Cell: Thanks. I am doing alright

1/2/18, 10:53 AM - Dwayne Taylor: Ok cool

1/2/18, 10:55 AM - Dwayne Taylor: Not trying to start no shit .. U seem to want to be left alone and I'm gonna so that. But I do have the money, tell me if u want me to just pay the bill give me the info...or send it pay pal?? Or whatevet Lemme know

1/2/18, 10:56 AM - Dwayne Taylor: Do not so

1/2/18, 11:21 AM - W Cell: Don't worry about it. Hold on to your money. I can handle the bill. Thank you.

1/2/18, 11:24 AM - Dwayne Taylor: But its not about that

1/2/18, 11:25 AM - Dwayne Taylor: I said I would

1/2/18, 11:25 AM - Dwayne Taylor: And I'm trying to

1/2/18, 11:26 AM - Dwayne Taylor: I did not forget that!

1/3/18, 5:09 PM - Dwayne Taylor: U need anything with the snow coming?

1/3/18, 5:41 PM - W Cell: I will be okay. Thanks for asking.

1/3/18, 6:02 PM - Dwayne Taylor: Aight

1/5/18, 4:03 PM - W Cell: https://www.google.com/amp/abc7ny.com/amp/off-duty-

police-lieutenant-struck-killed-while-helping-motorist/2866889/

1/5/18, 4:03 PM - W Cell: I knew him and his family

1/5/18, 4:07 PM - Dwayne Taylor: Oh wow... So sorry to hear

1/5/18, 4:11 PM - W Cell: What a shock. So sad

1/5/18, 4:13 PM - Dwayne Taylor: Yea it really is...wow

1/5/18, 4:37 PM - Dwayne Taylor: How r u?

1/5/18, 4:50 PM - W Cell: I am okay

1/5/18, 4:50 PM - W Cell: And u?

1/5/18, 4:50 PM - Dwayne Taylor: Good. I'm good thanks

1/5/18, 4:51 PM - W Cell: Good

1/6/18, 11:14 AM - Dwayne Taylor: Good morning. U ok?

1/6/18, 11:27 AM - W Cell: Hey. I'm okay. Thanks

1/6/18, 11:28 AM - W Cell: How are you?

1/6/18, 12:55 PM - Dwayne Taylor: Good thanks

1/7/18, 8:55 AM - Dwayne Taylor: Good morning. How r u today?

1/7/18, 10:43 AM - W Cell: Good morning. I'm ok and u?

1/7/18, 10:43 AM - Dwayne Taylor: I'm good thanks.

1/7/18, 11:04 AM - W Cell: Good

1/7/18, 11:04 AM - Dwayne Taylor: Can I see u this week?

1/7/18, 11:36 AM - W Cell: Yes

1/7/18, 1:03 PM - W Cell: What days do u work this week?

1/7/18, 1:04 PM - Dwayne Taylor: Thursday

1/8/18, 8:40 AM - Dwayne Taylor: Is it ok to come this morning?

1/8/18, 11:05 AM - W Cell: I am sorry. Just seeing this. Another day would be better. Work is busy.

1/8/18, 11:41 AM - Dwayne Taylor: No problem

1/8/18, 11:41 AM - Dwayne Taylor: How u feeling?

1/8/18, 11:54 AM - W Cell: I am ok. Was in some pain over the weekend, but better now.

1/8/18, 11:54 AM - W Cell: How r u?

1/8/18, 1:40 PM - Dwayne Taylor: Oh sorry to hear

1/8/18, 1:40 PM - Dwayne Taylor: I'm ok

1/8/18, 1:41 PM - Dwayne Taylor: Telling more movement?

1/8/18, 1:41 PM - Dwayne Taylor: Feeling

1/8/18, 3:22 PM - W Cell: Yes, feeling more but that doesn't cause pain

1/8/18, 3:28 PM - Dwayne Taylor: Oh nah didn't think that

1/9/18, 4:59 PM - Dwayne Taylor: Hello

1/9/18, 5:00 PM - Dwayne Taylor: Is tomm mid morning ok to stop by for a hot sec?

1/9/18, 7:29 PM - W Cell: Hey. I have phone meetings booked and not sure how long they will each take. Friday perhaps?

1/9/18, 7:42 PM - Dwayne Taylor: Ok

1/11/18, 12:42 PM - Dwayne Taylor: Hello

1/11/18, 1:14 PM - W Cell: Hey

1/11/18, 1:30 PM - Dwayne Taylor: How u?

1/11/18, 1:31 PM - W Cell: I'm okay and you?

1/11/18, 3:10 PM - Dwayne Taylor: I'm good thanks. Busy

1/11/18, 3:11 PM - Dwayne Taylor: We ok for tomm morning?

1/11/18, 8:35 PM - Dwayne Taylor: U ok?

1/11/18, 9:31 PM - W Cell: I am okay. I wasn't feeling great earlier.

1/11/18, 9:31 PM - Dwayne Taylor: Ok

1/11/18, 9:32 PM - Dwayne Taylor: Sorry to hear that

1/11/18, 9:32 PM - W Cell: Tomorrow morning will be tough for me...Work is crazy this week. We have a big deadline

1/11/18, 9:32 PM - Dwayne Taylor: Ohhh ok I understand

1/11/18, 9:32 PM - W Cell: Thanks....it just what it is

1/11/18, 9:32 PM - Dwayne Taylor: Another time

1/11/18, 9:32 PM - Dwayne Taylor: I would like to see u soon though

1/12/18, 4:03 PM - Dwayne Taylor: Hello

1/12/18, 4:08 PM - Dwayne Taylor: I don't like this tension between us. I don't like u not talking to me or us not talking, especially now. I would like to talk about it if you willing. Face to face

1/12/18, 7:34 PM - W Cell: Hey.

I'm not feeling tense. If you want to set up a time to talk, we can. What do u want to discuss?

1/12/18, 8:39 PM - Dwayne Taylor: How we are gonna proceed

1/12/18, 9:10 PM - W Cell: Ok

1/12/18, 9:21 PM - W Cell: I am proceeding by handling my priorities. That is all

1/12/18, 9:39 PM - Dwayne Taylor: Ok.

1/12/18, 9:40 PM - Dwayne Taylor: I don't have a problem with that. I'm talking about proceeding with my involvement

1/12/18, 9:40 PM - Dwayne Taylor: I will be involved

1/15/18, 2:57 PM - Dwayne Taylor: Hello

1/15/18, 3:15 PM - Dwayne Taylor: Wondering if I could stop by today for just a lil while

1/15/18, 4:44 PM - Dwayne Taylor: Well.. Hope u well

1/15/18, 5:14 PM - W Cell: Thanks, I am well. I had things lined up for today, including work. I wasn't expecting you to ask to stop by.

1/15/18, 5:15 PM - Dwayne Taylor: No prob

1/15/18, 5:21 PM - Dwayne Taylor: U free now?

1/15/18, 5:50 PM - Dwayne Taylor: How about weds after 3?

1/19/18, 7:15 AM - Dwayne Taylor: Hello hope all is well.

.

Are you going to tell me when you go into labor?

1/19/18, 9:14 AM - W Cell: Hi. Everything is going fine. Hope u are well too. At this point, I don't know when I will be going into labor. Still too early according to the doctor.

1/19/18, 10:02 AM - Dwayne Taylor: Are u going to tell me?

1/19/18, 10:02 AM - Dwayne Taylor: If like to be there

1/19/18, 10:02 AM - Dwayne Taylor: Id

1/19/18, 10:02 AM - Dwayne Taylor: If u dont mind

1/19/18, 11:46 AM - Dwayne Taylor: Can I see U today?

1/19/18, 11:59 AM - Dwayne Taylor: Or set next week please

1/19/18, 11:59 AM - Dwayne Taylor: Def

1/19/18, 1:08 PM - W Cell: Today isn't a good day. Next Tuesday or Wednesday would work for me.

1/19/18, 1:10 PM - Dwayne Taylor: Ill be there weds morning

1/19/18, 1:46 PM - Dwayne Taylor: Listen..u carrying my child.. And I would like to see u more!   Definitely more than not at all. You made it clear you don't wanna be in a relationship and I'm fine with that. But I don't wanna be denied things.. I wanna feel the baby kicking.

1/19/18, 1:46 PM - Dwayne Taylor: And I certainly wanna be there for the birth

1/19/18, 1:47 PM - Dwayne Taylor: I don't feel I've done anything to be denied any of this. I don't need to come around everyday... But I would sometimes

1/19/18, 11:45 PM - W Cell: "I don't feel I've done anything to be denied any of this." If that statement wasn't so ludicrous, it would be funny.

1/19/18, 11:53 PM - Dwayne Taylor: I haven't done anything to u

1/19/18, 11:53 PM - Dwayne Taylor: Nothing to make u not wanna communicate

1/19/18, 11:54 PM - Dwayne Taylor: U say that..with nothing at all to back it up...except some shit I didn't do at a hospital and some money I owe u from hotels

1/19/18, 11:55 PM - Dwayne Taylor: So u saying I wronged u so much I shouldn't be there to witness my child's birth?

1/19/18, 11:57 PM - W Cell: By your comments, you have not self reflected at all, perhaps u did and you don't have insight

1/19/18, 11:57 PM - W Cell: But I can't help with that

1/19/18, 11:58 PM - W Cell: I have not said anything to u about my birth plan or anything.

1/19/18, 11:58 PM - Dwayne Taylor: Yes I know...

1/20/18, 12:00 AM - Dwayne Taylor: I can't self reflect when I don't feel I've done anything to u

1/20/18, 12:00 AM - W Cell: You had time to think about things and that is all u see. I'm "upset" about money I never expected from you and ur disappointing behavior at the hospital

1/20/18, 12:00 AM - W Cell: Exaxtly

1/20/18, 12:00 AM - W Cell: Exactly

1/20/18, 12:00 AM - Dwayne Taylor: Listen...I dont need a lesson

1/20/18, 12:00 AM - W Cell: What u feel is just that...what u feel

1/20/18, 12:01 AM - W Cell: Neither do i

1/20/18, 12:01 AM - Dwayne Taylor: I can't feel what I don't understand

1/20/18, 12:02 AM - Dwayne Taylor: Yes... That's what I see cause that's all u explained to me

1/20/18, 12:02 AM - Dwayne Taylor: Ive been thinking..and yes... That's all I can see that in have done wrong

1/20/18, 12:02 AM - W Cell: Me trying to explain things to you is like 200 on my list of priorities right now

1/20/18, 12:03 AM - Dwayne Taylor: But I don't need u to explain anything... All I want is can I see u and am I gonna be informed u going into labor

1/20/18, 12:03 AM - Dwayne Taylor: U dont have to bother telling me everything I did wrong

1/20/18, 12:04 AM - Dwayne Taylor: At this point it ain't important

1/20/18, 12:05 AM - Dwayne Taylor: Watching tv

1/20/18, 12:05 AM - Dwayne Taylor: U?

1/20/18, 12:05 AM - W Cell: Text the wrong person?

1/20/18, 12:05 AM - Dwayne Taylor: Today was a great step

1/20/18, 12:05 AM - Dwayne Taylor: Oh sorry

1/20/18, 12:06 AM - Dwayne Taylor: U gonna answer the question?

1/20/18, 12:07 AM - Dwayne Taylor: Its simple questions

1/20/18, 12:08 AM - W Cell: I don't even know what to say but what a disappointment

1/20/18, 12:08 AM - Dwayne Taylor: As r u

1/20/18, 12:09 AM - Dwayne Taylor: Now just answer please

1/20/18, 12:11 AM - Dwayne Taylor: U don't have to be disappointed by me anymore....

1/20/18, 12:11 AM - Dwayne Taylor: That's all I seem to be to u ms. Perfect

1/20/18, 12:12 AM - W Cell: I am far from perfect. That is the truth.

1/20/18, 12:12 AM - Dwayne Taylor: There's really no need for all this... Just answer my questions.... Geez

1/20/18, 12:12 AM - Dwayne Taylor: That's all I need

1/20/18, 12:13 AM - W Cell: How about asking questions that would be helpful? And not centered on you feeling good

1/20/18, 12:13 AM - W Cell: You you you you and what u deserve

1/20/18, 12:13 AM - W Cell: Please

1/20/18, 12:14 AM - Dwayne Taylor: Hmmm.....

1/20/18, 12:14 AM - Dwayne Taylor: Really

1/20/18, 12:14 AM - W Cell: Feeling kicks? What about can I help do something? How are u? How are your doctor visits?

1/20/18, 12:14 AM - Dwayne Taylor: Oh my goodness

1/20/18, 12:15 AM - W Cell: I have re read some of the things u said and thought about what u said on the phone

1/20/18, 12:15 AM - Dwayne Taylor: Whitney.... I ask u every single time I texted how u were

1/20/18, 12:15 AM - W Cell: Rude

1/20/18, 12:15 AM - W Cell: Disrespectful

1/20/18, 12:15 AM - W Cell: Off basr

1/20/18, 12:15 AM - W Cell: Base

1/20/18, 12:15 AM - Dwayne Taylor: And u werent?

1/20/18, 12:16 AM - Dwayne Taylor: Whitney.... Every time I asked u could I do something for U u always say no

1/20/18, 12:16 AM - Dwayne Taylor: ALWAYS

1/20/18, 12:17 AM - Dwayne Taylor: I am not rude

1/20/18, 12:17 AM - W Cell: I have a whole lot to say about your "offers" to help

1/20/18, 12:17 AM - W Cell: Too much to text

1/20/18, 12:17 AM - W Cell: What a joke

1/20/18, 12:17 AM - Dwayne Taylor: Ummm... How would u when u don't accept

1/20/18, 12:17 AM - Dwayne Taylor: Nook ur the joke

1/20/18, 12:17 AM - Dwayne Taylor: Cause all this is funny

92

1/20/18, 12:18 AM - W Cell: Wow. Yup

1/20/18, 12:18 AM - Dwayne Taylor: Are u gonna sit here.... And say I never offered to do anything for u?

1/20/18, 12:19 AM - Dwayne Taylor: And the rare time u say yes do this for me and it doesn't get done?

1/20/18, 12:19 AM - W Cell: I didn't say u didn't offer...but there was always something to it

1/20/18, 12:19 AM - Dwayne Taylor: No there wasnt

1/20/18, 12:20 AM - W Cell: Ok

1/20/18, 12:20 AM - Dwayne Taylor: Perhaps U been jaded by other s

1/20/18, 12:20 AM - W Cell: Nope just your words

1/20/18, 12:20 AM - Dwayne Taylor: That I'm sure you took the wrong way u always do

1/20/18, 12:21 AM - Dwayne Taylor: Nothing I do... Or ever have tried to do is good enough for u

1/20/18, 12:22 AM - Dwayne Taylor: I constantly asked u could I do something for U?.. Or did u need anything... And u always said no

1/20/18, 12:22 AM - Dwayne Taylor: Y should I keep asking

1/20/18, 12:22 AM - Dwayne Taylor: Y!!???

1/20/18, 12:23 AM - Dwayne Taylor: And ur gonna sit here and tell me I'm asking to make myself feel good

1/20/18, 12:23 AM - W Cell: Dwayne, I could say so much but I won't. I'm sure u did what u could. Thanks

1/20/18, 12:23 AM - Dwayne Taylor: I go play with my dick to feel good!!#

1/20/18, 12:23 AM - Dwayne Taylor: Gettin rejected by u does not feel good to me

1/20/18, 12:23 AM - W Cell: Don't use that language with me

1/20/18, 12:24 AM - W Cell: Rejection doesn't feel good?

1/20/18, 12:24 AM - Dwayne Taylor: All u can say is bullshit

1/20/18, 12:24 AM - W Cell: That is not true at all

1/20/18, 12:25 AM - W Cell: I am not texting all of it because it is not the right forum and I don't feel it would make a difference

1/20/18, 12:25 AM - Dwayne Taylor: I've asked u to come over

Ice asked to do ur laundry

I've asked to take you to the doctor

1/20/18, 12:25 AM - Dwayne Taylor: Offered u food

1/20/18, 12:25 AM - Dwayne Taylor: I always get no

1/20/18, 12:25 AM - Dwayne Taylor: No no no

1/20/18, 12:25 AM - Dwayne Taylor: So y bother asking?

1/20/18, 12:26 AM - Dwayne Taylor: U don't want me around

1/20/18, 12:26 AM - Dwayne Taylor: And that's fine

1/20/18, 12:26 AM - Dwayne Taylor: Noooo.. The bullshit that ur gonna text isn't gonna make a difference

1/20/18, 12:27 AM - Dwayne Taylor: Cause I tried

1/20/18, 12:27 AM - W Cell: That actually made me laugh. Thanks

1/20/18, 12:27 AM - Dwayne Taylor: Good

1/20/18, 12:27 AM - Dwayne Taylor: Glad I can amuse u

1/20/18, 12:28 AM - Dwayne Taylor: But this brow beating.. That shit don't work on me

1/20/18, 12:28 AM - Dwayne Taylor: I don't give a Damn how u feel about me

1/20/18, 12:28 AM - Dwayne Taylor: Or what u think

1/20/18, 12:28 AM - Dwayne Taylor: Of me

1/20/18, 12:28 AM - Dwayne Taylor: I don't need ur approval

1/20/18, 12:29 AM - Dwayne Taylor: I didn't want any of this tonite

1/20/18, 12:29 AM - Dwayne Taylor: U shut me out... I didn't do that to u

1/20/18, 12:30 AM - Dwayne Taylor: But this ain't new... This what u do

1/20/18, 12:30 AM - Dwayne Taylor: All I wanted to know was two things

1/20/18, 12:30 AM - Dwayne Taylor: That s all

1/20/18, 12:31 AM - Dwayne Taylor: U don't want me around fine

1/20/18, 12:31 AM - W Cell: U didn't want this tonight but didn't think twice about interrupting me with those messages while I was working this afternoon. Right?

1/20/18, 12:31 AM - Dwayne Taylor: It was a text

1/20/18, 12:31 AM - W Cell: It isn't about u or wanting u around. I need peace serenity and support

1/20/18, 12:32 AM - Dwayne Taylor: Something u can answer at anytime

1/20/18, 12:32 AM - W Cell: That was distracting

1/20/18, 12:32 AM - Dwayne Taylor: Really

1/20/18, 12:32 AM - W Cell: Yes

1/20/18, 12:32 AM - W Cell: It was

1/20/18, 12:32 AM - Dwayne Taylor: Me saying can I come to the birth of my child really fucked up ur work flow??

1/20/18, 12:33 AM - Dwayne Taylor: Really?

1/20/18, 12:33 AM - Dwayne Taylor: I bet not one of the 8 calls ur mom made to u today distracted u

1/20/18, 12:33 AM - W Cell: It didn't but it shows a lack of consideration especially when I just said we could meet next week

1/20/18, 12:34 AM - W Cell: Why couldn't that wait?

1/20/18, 12:34 AM - W Cell: She didn't call as a matter of fact

1/20/18, 12:34 AM - W Cell: I'm top busy lately

1/20/18, 12:34 AM - W Cell: Too

1/20/18, 12:34 AM - Dwayne Taylor: It was a text

1/20/18, 12:34 AM - W Cell: I work 9 to 10 hours a day

1/20/18, 12:34 AM - Dwayne Taylor: Stop

1/20/18, 12:35 AM - Dwayne Taylor: U normally don't answer text until 5 hours later

98

1/20/18, 12:35 AM - Dwayne Taylor: Whitney

1/20/18, 12:35 AM - Dwayne Taylor: Its a simple yes or no

1/20/18, 12:36 AM - Dwayne Taylor: U don't want me around... No problem... But I will be around for my child

1/20/18, 12:37 AM - Dwayne Taylor: I have given u ur space

1/20/18, 12:37 AM - Dwayne Taylor: I don't bother you

1/20/18, 12:37 AM - Dwayne Taylor: U made it very clear u don't want me around.

1/20/18, 12:40 AM - Dwayne Taylor: U the last one need to be talking about consideration

1/20/18, 1:01 AM - Dwayne Taylor: I guess ur sleep.. Good nite.. Ill see you weds

1/20/18, 6:08 PM - Dwayne Taylor: Hello Whitney

1/20/18, 6:08 PM - Dwayne Taylor: Would u like to start over?

1/20/18, 10:00 PM - W Cell: In what way?

1/20/18, 10:01 PM - Dwayne Taylor: Reset button on our pregnancy relstionship

1/20/18, 10:01 PM - Dwayne Taylor: Relationship

1/20/18, 10:05 PM - Dwayne Taylor: Ur view of me too

1/21/18, 5:03 PM - W Cell: We can try if u want to

1/21/18, 5:08 PM - Dwayne Taylor: Do u want to?

1/21/18, 5:09 PM - Dwayne Taylor: Hello by the way. How are you?

1/21/18, 5:18 PM - W Cell: I'm Ok and u?

1/21/18, 5:18 PM - Dwayne Taylor: I'm good thanks.

1/21/18, 5:19 PM - Dwayne Taylor: R u ok?... Do u need anything?

1/21/18, 5:27 PM - W Cell: I'm okay. Just tired. I slept most of the day

1/21/18, 5:28 PM - W Cell: I am okay today, I don't need anything thanks

1/21/18, 5:28 PM - Dwayne Taylor: Ok

1/22/18, 9:36 AM - Dwayne Taylor: Hello

1/22/18, 9:36 AM - Dwayne Taylor: How u?

1/22/18, 10:05 AM - W Cell: Hey. I am okay. Same old aches and pains

1/22/18, 10:05 AM - W Cell: How r u?

1/22/18, 10:05 AM - Dwayne Taylor: Oh ok

1/22/18, 10:05 AM - Dwayne Taylor: I'm good

1/22/18, 10:06 AM - Dwayne Taylor: You ok. Think u gonna need anything?

1/22/18, 11:25 AM - W Cell: I'm okay. My mom is picking up my prescription on her way home so I'm good.

1/22/18, 11:25 AM - W Cell: I ordered a bassinet

1/22/18, 11:26 AM - W Cell: And of course it is like the most expensive one on the market....but it supposed to be the safest

1/22/18, 12:58 PM - Dwayne Taylor: Oh ok

1/22/18, 12:58 PM - Dwayne Taylor: I'm not surprised

1/22/18, 1:05 PM - W Cell: I requested delayed delivery so it won't be here for a while but I wanted to catch the sale.

1/22/18, 1:05 PM - Dwayne Taylor: I hear u

1/22/18, 3:11 PM - Dwayne Taylor: How much was it?

1/22/18, 3:27 PM - W Cell: Normal price is $1200 but I got it 40% off

1/22/18, 3:28 PM - Dwayne Taylor: Lol...whitney

1/22/18, 3:28 PM - Dwayne Taylor: Lol

1/22/18, 3:28 PM - W Cell: What?

1/22/18, 3:28 PM - Dwayne Taylor: Sooo u spent 700 dollars on a baby bed?

1/22/18, 3:30 PM - W Cell: It's a smart sleeper bassinet. It will last at least six months

1/22/18, 3:31 PM - Dwayne Taylor: U don't need to be smart to sleep...U only need to be tired!

1/22/18, 3:41 PM - W Cell: Sooo should I lol to the fact u had a car sitting there that couldn't be driven for a year? U paid more in two months for that than I did for this bed that may greatly enhance quality of life for baby and me. You laugh at me, not even asking about it's functionality or what makes it special. Smh.

1/22/18, 3:42 PM - Dwayne Taylor: Ummm... We talking about u right now

1/22/18, 3:42 PM - Dwayne Taylor: Y u always gotta bring up old stuff

1/22/18, 3:43 PM - Dwayne Taylor: What functions cannot perform?

1/22/18, 3:43 PM - Dwayne Taylor: Can't it

1/22/18, 3:43 PM - Dwayne Taylor: Can it

1/22/18, 3:43 PM - Dwayne Taylor: What functions can it perform

1/22/18, 3:57 PM - Dwayne Taylor: Was only mess in with u...

1/22/18, 3:57 PM - Dwayne Taylor: That bed is a bit pricy though

1/22/18, 4:29 PM - W Cell: Ok

1/22/18, 4:30 PM - Dwayne Taylor: Stop being so defensive....dag

1/22/18, 4:30 PM - Dwayne Taylor: U know imma mess with u

1/22/18, 4:30 PM - Dwayne Taylor: I could care less with what u spend ur money on

1/22/18, 4:31 PM - Dwayne Taylor: But really what good stuff can it do?

1/22/18, 7:39 PM - Dwayne Taylor: Hey

1/22/18, 7:39 PM - Dwayne Taylor: U aight?

1/22/18, 7:45 PM - W Cell: I am fine

1/22/18, 8:09 PM - Dwayne Taylor: Ok

1/22/18, 8:09 PM - Dwayne Taylor: Need ne thing?

1/22/18, 8:11 PM - Dwayne Taylor: How u tonite?

1/23/18, 10:00 AM - Dwayne Taylor: Good morning

1/23/18, 10:15 AM - W Cell: Hello

1/23/18, 11:06 AM - Dwayne Taylor: How u feeling?

1/23/18, 11:42 AM - W Cell: The same as usual. How are you?

1/23/18, 11:42 AM - Dwayne Taylor: I'm ok

1/23/18, 11:42 AM - Dwayne Taylor: Well... U been doin good

1/23/18, 11:43 AM - Dwayne Taylor: Soon u can have ur body back.

1/23/18, 11:43 AM - Dwayne Taylor: Hopefully not too soon though

1/23/18, 12:15 PM - W Cell: I have been feeling okay. Not great but there is no use in complaining. Right now I'm enjoying the quiet time.

1/23/18, 12:17 PM - Dwayne Taylor: Yea!!!... Do it now

1/23/18, 12:17 PM - Dwayne Taylor: Enjoy it now

1/23/18, 12:17 PM - Dwayne Taylor: What does the baby bed do?

1/23/18, 2:47 PM - W Cell: It's basically a robotic bed. It can replicate the sounds and motions of parent/caregiver. It is supposed to be the safest of its kind. Built in microphone so it can listen and adapt to baby needs including providing the right amount of motion and sound.

1/23/18, 2:48 PM - Dwayne Taylor: Hmmm

1/23/18, 2:48 PM - Dwayne Taylor: Ok

1/23/18, 3:20 PM - Dwayne Taylor: Wyd?

1/23/18, 3:37 PM - W Cell: Working

1/23/18, 3:37 PM - Dwayne Taylor: Yea

1/23/18, 4:14 PM - W Cell: So much to do

1/23/18, 4:31 PM - Dwayne Taylor: For work or in general?

1/23/18, 5:04 PM - W Cell: For work

1/23/18, 5:07 PM - Dwayne Taylor: Oh ok

1/23/18, 5:07 PM - Dwayne Taylor: Offer still on the table for me helping where I can

1/23/18, 5:07 PM - Dwayne Taylor: Just say something

1/25/18, 8:51 AM - Dwayne Taylor: Good morning

1/25/18, 9:11 AM - W Cell: Good morning

1/25/18, 9:11 AM - Dwayne Taylor: How you two doin?

1/25/18, 9:14 AM - W Cell: Ok. Very tired today

1/25/18, 9:14 AM - W Cell: How r u?

1/25/18, 9:15 AM - Dwayne Taylor: Oh sorry to hear...thinking of taking a nap for lunch break?.. I'm good thanks

1/25/18, 9:26 AM - Dwayne Taylor: Lot of work toda

1/25/18, 9:26 AM - Dwayne Taylor: Today

1/25/18, 9:29 AM - W Cell: Yes, lots of work. How about u?

1/25/18, 9:30 AM - Dwayne Taylor: Ohhh ok. I won't bother u.. Nah pretty light day. But yesterday was rough. U was my only break yesterday

1/25/18, 9:33 AM - W Cell: What did u have to do?

1/25/18, 9:34 AM - Dwayne Taylor: Meetings really

1/25/18, 2:12 PM - Dwayne Taylor: Do you need anything later?

1/25/18, 2:51 PM - W Cell: No thank you

1/25/18, 2:54 PM - Dwayne Taylor: Ok

1/26/18, 12:55 PM - Dwayne Taylor: Hey

1/26/18, 12:55 PM - Dwayne Taylor: How u?

1/26/18, 2:31 PM - W Cell: Hey. I'm okay. How are u?

1/26/18, 2:31 PM - Dwayne Taylor: I'm good.

1/26/18, 2:34 PM - W Cell: Good.

1/26/18, 2:35 PM - W Cell: How is the family?

1/26/18, 2:35 PM - Dwayne Taylor: Everyone is good.. How bout on ur end?

1/26/18, 2:35 PM - W Cell: Good

1/26/18, 2:38 PM - W Cell: What do u have going on?

1/26/18, 2:40 PM - Dwayne Taylor: I'm righting a letter to congress

1/26/18, 2:40 PM - Dwayne Taylor: Writing

1/26/18, 2:41 PM - W Cell: Ok nice

1/26/18, 2:41 PM - W Cell: What about?

1/26/18, 2:41 PM - Dwayne Taylor: Things the Vulcan do in the community

1/26/18, 2:42 PM - W Cell: Oh ok. Cool

1/26/18, 2:44 PM - Dwayne Taylor: U working I bet

1/26/18, 3:47 PM - W Cell: Yup. Everyday

1/26/18, 3:50 PM - Dwayne Taylor: Everyday??!

1/26/18, 4:00 PM - W Cell: Yes, I work everyday

1/26/18, 4:01 PM - Dwayne Taylor: Dang

As time went on communication became even shorter. I basically said hello to her and that was it. To this day, I don't know what I did wrong.

2/2/18, 2:49 PM - Dwayne Taylor: Yea.... So I guess U not gonna say Hi. So hello. How u?

2/2/18, 4:30 PM - W Cell: Hey. I'm good. How are you?

2/2/18, 4:31 PM - Dwayne Taylor: Good thanks.... You ain't so busy I can't get 10 secs Whitney

2/4/18, 8:41 PM - Dwayne Taylor: Ok... Well its obvious ur not gonna say hello to me. So how are you Whitney?

2/4/18, 8:41 PM - Dwayne Taylor: Hows peanut?

2/4/18, 9:20 PM - W Cell: As far as you know, I can't keep food down, I'm anemic and exhausted and working long hours in spite of it, it is painful for me to walk and stand. Yet, your big concern is that I don't say hi to you first. Seriously?

2/4/18, 9:20 PM - W Cell: Hello. I'm okay and hope u are well

2/4/18, 9:26 PM - Dwayne Taylor: Whit. There's nothing I can do to help with that. I get that and if I could help I would.. But why am I always what can be sacrificed?

2/4/18, 9:26 PM - Dwayne Taylor: Nothing us going to stop what u going through

2/4/18, 9:27 PM - Dwayne Taylor: I was only asking for a 5 second text

2/4/18, 9:27 PM - Dwayne Taylor: Since christmas

2/4/18, 9:28 PM - Dwayne Taylor: And no you saying hello is not my biggest concern. But there's nothing I can do for you. Specially if you don't allow it

2/4/18, 9:30 PM - Dwayne Taylor: But I didn't text to upset u. Have a good night

2/5/18, 9:25 AM - Dwayne Taylor: Morning. How are you? Do you need anything?

2/5/18, 10:34 AM - W Cell: Hello. I'm okay. How are u? No, thanks.

2/5/18, 10:35 AM - Dwayne Taylor: Good thanks

2/5/18, 11:33 AM - W Cell: Good

2/5/18, 2:59 PM - Dwayne Taylor: Did u figure out if u wanted me to go with u to get ur IV?

2/5/18, 3:17 PM - W Cell: I'm still working on a date

2/5/18, 3:17 PM - Dwayne Taylor: Ok

2/5/18, 3:51 PM - Dwayne Taylor: Would u like to be my Valentine?

2/6/18, 9:43 AM - Dwayne Taylor: Hello. How are you today?. Need ne thing?

2/6/18, 2:56 PM - W Cell: Hey. I'm having some issues but ok. Work is busy too

2/6/18, 2:57 PM - Dwayne Taylor: Ok

2/7/18, 1:28 PM - Dwayne Taylor: Hello. How r u?

2/7/18, 1:45 PM - W Cell: Hey. I'm okay. I was in the hospital for a few hours this morning. On my way home now. How are you?

2/7/18, 1:46 PM - Dwayne Taylor: What happened?

2/7/18, 1:46 PM - Dwayne Taylor: U ok?

2/7/18, 2:12 PM - W Cell: The doctor wanted me in for testing and fluids via iv. Tests came back clear. I was a bit dehydrated. Got a new prescription.

2/7/18, 2:13 PM - Dwayne Taylor: Oh ok

2/7/18, 2:13 PM - Dwayne Taylor: Glad u ok

2/7/18, 3:12 PM - W Cell: Thank you

2/7/18, 3:13 PM - W Cell: Back home now

2/7/18, 3:13 PM - Dwayne Taylor: Good

2/7/18, 3:22 PM - Dwayne Taylor: I actually thought u were home for a while now

2/7/18, 3:26 PM - W Cell: it takes a while to get from the hospital

2/7/18, 3:26 PM - Dwayne Taylor: Ok. U need ne thing?

2/7/18, 9:04 PM - W Cell: No thanks. Still sick but I will deal with that tomorrow

2/7/18, 9:18 PM - Dwayne Taylor: Ok

2/8/18, 12:52 PM - Dwayne Taylor: Hello. How are u today?

2/8/18, 1:47 PM - W Cell: Hey. I'm okay. How are you?

2/8/18, 1:49 PM - Dwayne Taylor: I'm good thanks

2/8/18, 1:57 PM - W Cell: Working?

2/8/18, 2:16 PM - Dwayne Taylor: Yes

2/8/18, 8:27 PM - Dwayne Taylor: Can I see u tomm?

2/10/18, 11:50 AM - Dwayne Taylor: Hello?

2/10/18, 1:01 PM - W Cell: Hey

2/10/18, 1:02 PM - Dwayne Taylor: Are u aight? U ain't been answering lately

2/10/18, 1:10 PM - W Cell: Sorry about about missing your last question. I'm okay just a lot going on. Did I miss something else? How are you?

2/10/18, 1:14 PM - Dwayne Taylor: Nah it wasn't important

2/10/18, 1:14 PM - Dwayne Taylor: I'm ok thanks

2/10/18, 1:14 PM - Dwayne Taylor: Are u ok?

2/10/18, 1:17 PM - W Cell: I'm the same. My mother is under the weather too

2/10/18, 1:18 PM - Dwayne Taylor: Sorry to hear

2/10/18, 1:20 PM - W Cell: Thanks it's ok

2/10/18, 1:20 PM - Dwayne Taylor: Need anything?

2/10/18, 3:59 PM - W Cell: I'm fine thanks

2/10/18, 4:00 PM - Dwayne Taylor: Ok

2/10/18, 4:07 PM - W Cell: Having a good weekend so far?

2/10/18, 4:08 PM - Dwayne Taylor: Its ok... Just came back from a presentation. Other than that just chillin. How about u?

2/10/18, 4:13 PM - W Cell: Nice. Mine is okay

2/10/18, 4:13 PM - Dwayne Taylor: Ok.

2/10/18, 4:14 PM - Dwayne Taylor: Good

2/10/18, 4:30 PM - Dwayne Taylor: U gonna need anything for ur ma?

2/10/18, 4:39 PM - W Cell: No, thanks

2/10/18, 4:39 PM - W Cell: How is your mom?

2/10/18, 4:39 PM - Dwayne Taylor: Ok.

2/10/18, 4:40 PM - Dwayne Taylor: She's good

2/11/18, 1:19 PM - Dwayne Taylor: Hello. How u?

2/11/18, 1:23 PM - W Cell: Hi. I'm ok. How are you?

2/11/18, 1:26 PM - Dwayne Taylor: I'm good. Need anything later?

2/11/18, 1:50 PM - W Cell: Good. No, thank you.

2/11/18, 1:50 PM - Dwayne Taylor: Ok

2/12/18, 1:33 PM - Dwayne Taylor: Hello Whitney... How are you today?

2/12/18, 4:45 PM - W Cell: Hey. I'm okay. Went to the doctor. How are you?

2/12/18, 4:57 PM - Dwayne Taylor: Oh which doc?

2/12/18, 4:58 PM - Dwayne Taylor: U ok?

2/12/18, 5:35 PM - W Cell: The hemotologist. I'm okay.

2/12/18, 5:45 PM - Dwayne Taylor: Ok

2/13/18, 9:31 AM - Dwayne Taylor: Hello Whitney

2/13/18, 9:32 AM - Dwayne Taylor: How r u?

2/13/18, 11:46 AM - W Cell: Hey. I'm okay. Super busy with work. Wish I didn't have to do it. I just don't have the energy

2/13/18, 11:47 AM - W Cell: How are you?

2/13/18, 12:01 PM - Dwayne Taylor: I'm ok

2/13/18, 12:01 PM - Dwayne Taylor: Can I stop by for a quick sec tomm?

2/15/18, 5:35 PM - Dwayne Taylor: Hello. How are you today?

2/15/18, 7:01 PM - W Cell: Hey. I'm ok. How are you?

2/15/18, 7:01 PM - Dwayne Taylor: Good thanks

2/16/18, 12:43 PM - Dwayne Taylor: Hello how are you?

2/16/18, 1:07 PM - W Cell: Hey. I'm good thanks for asking. How are you?

2/16/18, 1:26 PM - Dwayne Taylor: Good thanks

2/16/18, 2:02 PM - W Cell: Good

2/17/18, 1:12 PM - Dwayne Taylor: Hello. How r u?

2/17/18, 2:13 PM - W Cell: Hey. I'm ok and u?

2/17/18, 2:41 PM - Dwayne Taylor: I'm good thanks

2/18/18, 2:09 PM - Dwayne Taylor: Hey. How r u today?

2/18/18, 4:50 PM - W Cell: Hey. I'm okay and you?

2/18/18, 5:08 PM - Dwayne Taylor: I'm good

2/19/18, 9:12 AM - Dwayne Taylor: Good morning. How are you today?

2/19/18, 10:06 AM - W Cell: Hi. I'm good and you?

2/19/18, 10:07 AM - Dwayne Taylor: I'm good thanks

2/20/18, 9:52 AM - Dwayne Taylor: Good morning. How are u?

If you notice, son, there is something special about this day. This is the day you were born. However, at that time I didn't know you were born. This is also the first time she didn't respond to a morning text. I thought it was odd but as you just read there were times she flat out didn't respond to text, so I didn't think all that much about it. I figured she was busy or just didn't want to talk to me, so I would just reach out the next day.

2/21/18, 7:38 AM - Dwayne Taylor: Whit.. U ok?

117

2/21/18, 7:50 AM - W Cell: I'm doing okay. Thank you. How are you?

2/21/18, 7:52 AM - Dwayne Taylor: I'm good thanks. You need anything?

2/21/18, 9:38 AM - W Cell: No, I'm okay. Thank you for asking.

2/21/18, 10:09 AM - Dwayne Taylor: Ok

She had you. On February 20, 2018! And made no mention of your arrival for 6 DAYS!!! Even though I spoke to her every day!

2/22/18, 10:05 AM - Dwayne Taylor: Hello. How are you today?

2/22/18, 11:49 AM - W Cell: Hey. I'm okay, thanks. And you?

2/22/18, 11:53 AM - Dwayne Taylor: I'm good thanks

2/23/18, 8:40 AM - Dwayne Taylor: Hello. How are you today?

2/23/18, 8:58 AM - Dwayne Taylor: Whit?

2/23/18, 8:59 AM - Dwayne Taylor: U have to go to Lamaze classes or something?

2/23/18, 4:02 PM - Dwayne Taylor: Well I hope u are ok

2/24/18, 11:23 AM - Dwayne Taylor: Whit are u ok?

2/25/18, 1:31 PM - Dwayne Taylor: Hello?

2/26/18, 12:25 PM - W Cell: Hi, Dwayne. I see that you asked about Lamaze classes. It is a bit too late, and besides, I couldn't do it anyway.

I went to the hospital again with some symptoms. It was immediately apparent that the baby was in distress. An emergency C-section was performed. I delivered a baby boy.

It happened very quickly. No labor just delivery. I was in total shock and couldn't handle additional drama or stress brought on by anyone. Plus I'm in a great deal of physical pain. I'm sure you would like to see the baby. Text me if you are coming today and what time. Please note no other visitors are allowed. The hospital is St. Joseph's University Regional Hospital. The address is...

2/26/18, 1:14 PM - Dwayne Taylor: Yes i will be there today!

2/26/18, 1:14 PM - Dwayne Taylor: I'm coming now!

When I got to the hospital, I didn't want to argue. I wasn't even upset, I was just happy both of you were okay. When I first got the text, I thought your mom had gone to the hospital that morning. But then I noticed she was walking around the unit with her plain clothes on, not a hospital robe. So I asked her when you were born, and she confessed that you were born 6 days prior. I was puzzled, I didn't question her about it; and it didn't matter at that time because you were here, and I was happy. I thought things would start to go back to normal, I missed my friend. I thought she would go back to being that woman with whom I fell in love. But I was wrong.

That time at the hospital was nice. I met you for the first time and held you. I felt all those things I felt when I held your sister and brother for the first time. Thoughts of…who you were going to be? Who were you going to be more like? What were you going to like? What was going to be your favorite food? What were you going to like to do? How long were you going to keep me up at night? What was going to be your favorite subject in school? What was going to be your favorite cartoon or TV show? What was going to be your favorite toy? What college? How was I going to start saving for college? There were a million thoughts and questions. I thought of it all in just those 2 hours I held you.

The mood at this time was good with your mother. After visiting you, I dropped her off at a doctor's office. Your grandmother was suffering from a bad cold, then. During the car ride I still didn't question her on why she waited 6 days to tell me you were here. I was in a good place and didn't want to spoil it by bringing any negativity up. As far as I was concerned, it was the past. I just wanted to move forward and plan on seeing you the next day.

2/27/18, 5:43 PM - Dwayne Taylor: How are u?

2/27/18, 6:47 PM - W Cell: I'm okay. I just got my phone back. It's been a rough day.

2/27/18, 6:48 PM - Dwayne Taylor: Well relax tonite. Ill be there at 9 tomm

2/27/18, 7:21 PM - W Cell: I'm at the medical center with my mother tonight. She should be released tomorrow morning. I saw the baby briefly and dropped off milk when I went to my doctor's appointment this afternoon. Tomorrow, I plan to get to the hospital between 1 and 2pm.

2/27/18, 7:22 PM - W Cell: You can meet me there

2/27/18, 7:23 PM - Dwayne Taylor: I gotta see if I can see him earlier. Cause injave to leave at 4. I have a class

2/27/18, 7:23 PM - Dwayne Taylor: I was hoping u was there tonight

2/27/18, 7:23 PM - Dwayne Taylor: But ok

2/27/18, 7:24 PM - Dwayne Taylor: U need anything for U n ur mom?

I wanted to see you that next day, which was 2-27-18, but your mom and grandmother never made it home that night because your grandmother had to be admitted to the hospital. I had some chores to do and errands to run so I figured I would get all my work done for the week so I could spend more time with you. The following day (2-28-18), I had scheduled a class for the evening so I planned on seeing you that morning and spending as much time as I could before my class which I did convey to your mother. When I arrived at the hospital I was admitted to the unit where you were without any issues although the nurse at the desk told me I needed some kind of a bracelet. Another nurse there recognized me from two days prior, so I was allowed in.

I was exceedingly happy to be there with you. You were still sleeping and had rolled up blankets on your arms and tubes in you because you were born prematurely and certain organs in your body weren't fully developed, including your digestive system. I urgently wanted to get there and be with you because the day I was there, there were a few babies there alone and I didn't like that. I didn't want you to be there alone, especially with your mom looking after your grandmother.

The nurse led me in the ICU and put you in my arms. I remember being a little nervous when she gave you to me because you were so tiny and fragile. The nurse was still concerned that I didn't have a bracelet to get in, so just to be on the safe side she called your mother to make sure she was aware. When she called your mom, she didn't answer the phone, so the nurse left a message.

As I watched you sleep, again many thoughts ran through my head. I thought of taking you to the park, taking you to Disney to see Mickey Mouse, and having talks about girls. I was sitting with you for about an hour when the nurse came back in the room and started moving things around at your station. I didn't think anything of it, assuming she was doing what she normally did. When all of a sudden, she turned to me and said, "I have to take the baby from you. His mother called back, and she wants you to leave." I asked the nurse to repeat herself because I thought I heard something wrong. She repeated herself, and I asked the nurse, "What is going on here?!" The nurse responded, "I think you and his mother need to talk." I didn't cause a scene, nor did I yell at the nurse. I gave you back to the nurse and left.

I was absolutely heart broken and confused. I didn't know what the hell was going on. I didn't even make it off the floor before I called your mother. Of course, she didn't answer the phone. So I texted her:

2/28/18, 10:35 AM - Dwayne Taylor: Yo

2/28/18, 10:37 AM - Dwayne Taylor: What is going on??

2/28/18, 10:47 AM - Dwayne Taylor: Im sitting up there with him. And you called them and ask the to tell me to

leave!. I came here so he wouldn't be alone! Cause I
know u was with ur mother. Why would you do that?

2/28/18, 11:03 AM - W Cell: The hospital called me to let
me know someone that I didn't authorize was with
William. I called and followed up. I said that you could
finish your visit but to explain the rules to you upon your
leaving. No one can be bedside without me, which I
already relayed to you. I must be present. You are
welcome to visit anytime when I am visiting. I told plan
for today. Going forward, I will have a more planned
visiting schedule from which we can coordinate. That
should help.

She was aware I was going to be there, and she never told
me that no one could be with you without her present.
Why? Why couldn't anyone be in the hospital with you
without her there? I would have questioned why I couldn't
be there without her. I am your father! Who better than me
to protect you? That is no hospital rule I have ever read.
And if that was the rule, why didn't the nurses tell me that
when I arrived? What she told me was unacceptable and
she was lying. That nurse came in the unit and immediately
asked me to leave. She would only do that with explicit
detail from your mother.

2/28/18, 11:38 AM - Dwayne Taylor: No

2/28/18, 11:38 AM - Dwayne Taylor: You told them to ask
me to leave!

124

2/28/18, 11:38 AM - Dwayne Taylor: Why do I need you to see my son?

2/28/18, 11:38 AM - Dwayne Taylor: I want the other braclet

2/28/18, 11:39 AM - Dwayne Taylor: Your mother doesn't need it... She will always be with u

2/28/18, 11:40 AM - Dwayne Taylor: They didn't tell me I could finish the visit! They told me I had to leave and you told them to do that!

2/28/18, 11:41 AM - Dwayne Taylor: Your going up there today... Leave the bracelet or tell them to deactivate your mothers

2/28/18, 11:42 AM - Dwayne Taylor: If you don't wanna leave the bracelet with them I can Pick it up from you tomm morning!

2/28/18, 11:43 AM - Dwayne Taylor: Or I can go to the hospital to get it directly from your mother. Which ever works for yall

2/28/18, 11:44 AM - Dwayne Taylor: I have been calm and reserved through all this so as not to stress U. But them ripping him out my arms telling me u authorized that pissed me off!

2/28/18, 11:45 AM - Dwayne Taylor: Your bullshit stops today!!

2/28/18, 11:45 AM - Dwayne Taylor: I am not threatening you... I am not going to cause you any physical harm

2/28/18, 11:45 AM - Dwayne Taylor: But something is not right about this whole thing

2/28/18, 12:14 PM - W Cell: For the time being, all visitors, including my mother, will have to visit with me present. The only "activated" bracelet at this time is mine. You can visit with me. If you want to discuss this, we can schedule a time to talk.

2/28/18, 12:15 PM - Dwayne Taylor: Well tell them to activate another one for me. There's nothing to talk about concerning that. Why we even going through this right now is ridiculous

2/28/18, 12:16 PM - Dwayne Taylor: Why do I need your permission or authorization to see my own son?!

2/28/18, 12:17 PM - Dwayne Taylor: I went up there so he wouldn't be alone!

2/28/18, 12:17 PM - Dwayne Taylor: Why do I need U to sit with him?

2/28/18, 12:19 PM - Dwayne Taylor: I am not waiting to talk to U about this. Cause it ain't gonna happen All you have to do is give me my bracelet.

2/28/18, 12:19 PM - Dwayne Taylor: No need to talk about this

Your mother and I have always had an intricate relationship. There was always some confusion and things not said. But I always thought there was a great amount of love and respect between us. When the relationship started again, I tried to fix the negative issues suffered in the past. I thought I was clear on my motives, more vocal on how I felt, and included her in more aspects of my life. But the last few months of your mother's pregnancy it appeared she was going out of her way to push me away. According to her...I couldn't do anything right and I wanted to be with my ex. Then, I got the silent treatment. I thought she was going through something hormonal or emotional, and thought it would end after you were born. But now she is trying to keep me away from you.

Why?! What is going on here?! There was only one logical explanation for all of this. So I asked the big question:

2/28/18, 12:24 PM - Dwayne Taylor: Yo.... Is it possible that someone else is the father of this child Whitney?

2/28/18, 12:36 PM - Dwayne Taylor: If he is not... I will not harm you.. I will not talk bad about u. I will walk away and never bother you again

I had to ask her if I was your father. It is the only thing that would explain all these actions. To me, it was the only logical answer. This was the first time in a long time I asked your mom a question and she actually gave me a direct answer.

2/28/18, 2:59 PM - W Cell: Yes, I believe someone else is the father. Thank you for understanding a difficult situation.

"Thank you for understanding a difficult situation." That's all I got. No explanation, no apologies for putting me through mental or emotional hell for months. Worrying about her and you every day for months, just to tell me she believes someone else is your father. Why not maybe mention this one time in the midst of all the arguments?

Discovering this was extremely hurtful. Everything I was doing was for nothing. I tried so hard to do things right in order to be with her. As I said before, I tried to fix all the problems she had with the relationship in the past. She said I didn't include her in friend or family gatherings, that she was my "secret". I fixed that by inviting her to every single family gathering I had. I invited her to holiday parties, friend's birthday parties and award ceremonies. She said I didn't "talk to her" or include her in my future plans. I told her I wanted to marry her and start a family with her. I told her this while we looked for houses to live in.

All this meant absolutely nothing to her, and not once did she stop me and say, "Listen…there's a chance this child may not be yours." She just let me keep going. Instead of being an adult and saying she didn't want to be together or that you weren't mine, she tried to blame me for not doing things right and push me away.

I wasn't convinced you weren't mine. I also had a conversation with my mom about it. She was hurt as well. She said, "Something just isn't right." She felt I should still ask for a paternity test, which I wanted to do anyway.

2/28/18, 3:06 PM - Dwayne Taylor: Well we need an immediate paternity test

2/28/18, 3:26 PM - Dwayne Taylor: I have a test we can do this tomm or friday

2/28/18, 10:16 PM - Dwayne Taylor: Whitney

2/28/18, 10:16 PM - Dwayne Taylor: This is not going to linger.

2/28/18, 10:20 PM - Dwayne Taylor: Or did u get a test done already and u are certain hes not mine

3/1/18, 9:55 AM - Dwayne Taylor: Whitney...

3/1/18, 9:55 AM - Dwayne Taylor: I wanna resolve this issue

3/1/18, 9:56 AM - Dwayne Taylor: I can be at the hospital tomm.

3/1/18, 9:56 AM - Dwayne Taylor: With the test

3/1/18, 3:09 PM - Dwayne Taylor: I know you are getting these messages...I know u look at ur phone every 20 damn seconds! I really don't know what I've done to U to make u react this way toward me.

3/1/18, 3:10 PM - Dwayne Taylor: I have been very understanding through all u have put me through this passed few months. All I'm asking is for some understanding on your part.

3/1/18, 3:11 PM - Dwayne Taylor: U made it crystal clear u don't want me around

3/1/18, 3:13 PM - Dwayne Taylor: So all I'm asking is u do one last thing and let me and William take a paternity

*test. And if I'm not the father like u think I promise you
will never hear from me again*

*3/2/18, 12:02 PM - W Cell: As I have told you, you are not
the father. Paternity has been established.*

3/2/18, 12:55 PM - Dwayne Taylor: No U didnt

*3/2/18, 12:55 PM - Dwayne Taylor: U said U don't believe
I am*

*3/2/18, 12:55 PM - Dwayne Taylor: I still would like my
own testing done.*

3/2/18, 12:55 PM - Dwayne Taylor: If we can do that

*3/2/18, 1:14 PM - Dwayne Taylor: Or could you email me
the test results*

*3/2/18, 2:12 PM - Dwayne Taylor: Hello? I can be there
tomm*

*3/2/18, 10:37 PM - Dwayne Taylor: Whitney why did you
do this to me?*

The problem was when your mother told me I wasn't your
father, she basically took away any power I had. There was
nothing I could do. I couldn't visit you in the hospital, I
couldn't show you off to family, and I couldn't even put
you on my insurance. She was allowed to do all this just by

131

word of mouth. To this day, I don't think she even put me on your birth certificate. Feeling helpless, I called the hospital to asked them what I could do. The person I spoke to told me the only thing I could do was seek legal representation. So, that is what I did.

NJ DIVORCE SOLUTIONS

PREVITE NACHLINGER PC

LITIGATION	MEDIATION	CONSULTING

Thomas J. Bean, Esq.
Anthony W. Dunleavy, Esq.
John Nachlinger, Esq. [1,2,3]
Christina Previte, Esq.

[1] Certified by NJ Supreme Court as a Matrimonial Attorney
[2] Admitted in New York
[3] Admitted before the U.S. Supreme Court

128 Wood Ave. South, Suite 602
Iselin, NJ 08830
Phone: (732) 529-6937
Fax: (732) 909-2701
centraljerseyfamilylaw.com

March 9, 2018

Whitney English
XXXX
XXXX

    Re: *Dwayne Taylor v. Whitney English*

Dear Ms. English:

    My office represents Mr. Taylor in a paternity action. If you have retained counsel or intend to, kindly forward this letter to your attorney.

    My client has filed a complaint with the Hudson County Superior Court seeking to establish paternity of William English. You have advised Mr. Taylor that paternity was established and that he is not the child's biological father. Kindly forward the results of this paternity test to my office via fax, regular mail, or email to anthony@pnlawnj.com. If it is established that Mr. Taylor is not the child's father, then my client will withdraw his complaint. Mr. Taylor would like to resolve this matter amicably and I ask that you work with us in doing so.

    If you or your attorney have any questions or concerns, please email me. Please be advised that I cannot provide legal advice.

                     Very truly yours,
                     NJ DIVORCE SOLUTIONS

                     Anthony W. Dunleavy, Esq.

CC: Dwayne Taylor (via MyCase only)

Anthony W. Dunleavy, Esq. (038412010)
Previte Nachlinger, P.C.
120 Wood Ave. South, Suite 602
Iselin, New Jersey 08830
(732) 529-6937
Attorneys for Plaintiff, Dwayne Taylor

DWAYNE TAYLOR, Plaintiff, v. WHITNEY ENGLISH, Defendant.	**SUPERIOR COURT OF NEW JERSEY** **CHANCERY DIVISION – FAMILY PART** **HUDSON COUNTY** **DOCKET NO: FD** **Civil Action** **CONSENT ORDER**

This matter being brought before the above Court by the Plaintiff, DWAYNE TAYLOR, represented by Anthony W. Dunleavy, Esq. of Previte Nachlinger, P.C., and the Defendant, WHITNEY ENGLISH, represented by Jenny Berse, Esq. of Berse Law L.L.C., and it appearing that the parties have reached an agreement as to various issues regarding the paternity, custody, parenting time, and child support of William English, born February 20, 2018 (hereafter "minor child"), and it is for good cause shown;

It is on this ____ day of _____ 2018 ORDERED as follows:

1.   The parties acknowledge that the Plaintiff and Defendant engaged in a dating relationship around the time the Defendant became pregnant with William English, who was born on February 20, 2018. It is the intent of the parties to establish paternity of William. Plaintiff and Defendant will make arrangements to complete a "2 Party Legal Paternity Test" on-site at LabCorp, located at 600 Pavonia Ave, Ground Level, Jersey City, NJ 07306. Plaintiff and William shall be tested no later than April 30, 2018.

134

The anticipated cost is $525, which the parties will share equally. If either party advances the full amount, then the other party shall reimburse within five (5) days. The Plaintiff shall be entitled to be present when the test is administered to William. The Defendant shall provide notice to the Plaintiff five (5) days before William's test is to be administered.

2.   LabCorp shall forward the paternity test results to Plaintiff and Defendant.

3.   If the results are such that the Plaintiff is determined to be William's biological father, then the parties shall first discuss issues of custody, parenting time, and child support, if applicable, before filing an application with the court. If the parties cannot reach an agreement regarding custody, parenting time, or child support, then the parties shall attend mediation before filing an application with the court.

4.   Plaintiff and Defendant shall each pay their respective legal fees in connection with Plaintiff's application to establish paternity filed March 12, 2018.

_____
J.S.C.

_____
DWAYNE TAYLOR
Plaintiff

Date:

_____
ANTHONY W. DUNLEAVY, ESQ.
Attorney for Plaintiff

Date:

_____
WHITNEY ENGLISH
Defendant

Date:

_____
JENNY BERSE, ESQ.
Attorney for Defendant

Date:

On March 7, 2018, I had a meeting with a lawyer to find out what I could do in order to see you and find out what rights I had. There weren't many things I could do at this stage, all I could really do is ask the court to have a paternity test done, which is all I truly wanted anyway. I figured once I proved what I already knew (that you were my son) I would at least be able to see you and bring you to my house to see your family once a week. But that didn't happen. In fact, nothing happened for about 3 months. Your mother did nothing. Even after I contacted her, asking her to get the test done. It got to the point where I had to threaten to take her to court in order for her to get a simple test done. This is when the games started. Once a week, I heard from my lawyer telling me your mother was going to sign a consent order and get the test done. But she didn't do that either. After a couple months or so, I filed a motion in the court.

DWAYNE TAYLOR
_____
Plaintiff

vs.

WHITNEY ENGLISH
_____
Defendant

COUNTY: HUDSON

DOCKET NO.: FD - _____

CS NO: _____

CIVIL ACTION

Verified Complaint or
Counterclaim

I, Dwayne Taylor _____ by way of verified complaint/counterclaim, I certify the following:

1. I am the ☒ Plaintiff ☐ Defendant in the above-captioned matter.

2. Plaintiff resides at: Address: 100 South Inman Avenue

   City/Town: Avenel

   County: Middlesex   State: NJ   Zip Code: 07001

   Defendant resides at: Address: Parkside East, 30 Newport Parkway, Apt 2112

   City/Town: Jersey City

   County: Hudson   State: NJ   Zip Code: 07310

3. The child(ren) pertaining to this complaint are:

Name	Date of Birth	M/F	Residing at	Residing with (relationship)
WILLIAM	02/20/2016	M	Parkside East, 30 Newport Parkway, Apt 2112, JC, NJ	Mother

4. Other interested parties' name(s) and address(es).

_____

_____

_____

I have been previously been involved in the following family court actions with regard to any of the parties or children listed above. (If yes, give the title of case and docket number.)
☐ Yes   ☐ No

   Title of Case (_____ vs. _____)   Docket Number

   a. _____   _____

   b. _____   _____

   c. _____   _____

137

5. A Child Protection Agency (i.e. the Division of Youth and Family Services) (or a similar agency in another State) has been involved with the child(ren) or listed parties.
   ☐ Yes   ☐ No

6. This is an active public assistance case governed by 41 U.S.C.A. 602 (A) (26), N.J.S.A. 44: 10-1.1, et seq
   ☐ Yes   ☐ No

7. I seek the following for the child(ren) named on page 1.

   ■ Establish Paternity   ☐ Establish Maternity

   ■ Custody
      ■ Joint Legal Custody   ☐ Sole Legal Custody   ☐ Physical Custody

   ☐ Support Order: I am seeking the establishment of a court order against the person who is the spouse/civil union or domestic partner and/or parent of the persons listed on page 1 and has a legal duty to support same pursuant to N.J.S.A. 9:17-38 et seq. Chapter 92. The law requires that child support provisions of court orders shall be enforced by immediate income withholding upon the obligor's current or future income due from an employer or future employer, unemployment compensation or income from any source unless the obligor and obligee agree, in writing to an alternative arrangement or either party demonstrates and the court finds good cause for establishing an alternative arrangement (N.J.S.A. 2A: 17-56.9). For the reason(s) checked below, the defendant is under a legal duty to support and maintain the person(s) mentioned on page 1 of this complaint

      ☐ Plaintiff/Defendant is my lawful wife/husband/domestic partner/civil union partner
      ☐ Plaintiff/Defendant is the biological mother/father of the child(ren) named on page 1

   Reason for seeking custody and/or support:
   _____
   _____
   _____
   _____

   ■ Establish court ordered parenting time arrangements:
      ■ Parenting Time   ☐ Grandparent Time   ☐ Sibling Time

   Reasons for requesting court ordered parenting time arrangements:
   Please see Plaintiff's Certification attached hereto
   _____
   _____
   _____

   ☐ Medical Coverage Requested:
      ☐ Health Benefits for myself
      ☐ Health Benefits for the child(ren) named in this complaint

138

■ Other Relief Requested. Explain the relief being sought. Use additional information sheet, if necessary.

Please see Plaintiff's Certification attached hereto

_____

_____

_____

Required Attachments:
☐ A Certificate of Parentage is attached (if available)

☐ Certification to Establish Paternity attached (when seeking establishment of paternity)

I certify that the foregoing statements made by me are true. I am aware that if any of the foregoing statements made by me are willfully false, I am subject to punishment.

05/25/2018
Date   Signature plaintiff/counterclaimant

_____   _____
Date   Signature Co-plaintiff/Co-defendant

Court Appearance Information

Your appearance is mandatory. You may bring an attorney, although an attorney is not required. If you require assistance in selecting an attorney, you may contact your County Bar Association. If you cannot afford an attorney, you may contact Legal Services of New Jersey at www.lsnj.org. You may file a written response by certification opposing this complaint/cross complaint. Any written response you send to the Court must be sent to the other party. Your written response must be filed with the court and served on the other party at least 15 **DAYS PRIOR** to the hearing date. If you fail to appear at the hearing, an Order granting the relief requested by the filing party may be granted although your written response, if filed, will be considered. If you are the filer of this complaint you may file a certification in support of your complaint which shall not exceed **fifteen (15)** pages. If you are the person served with this complaint/cross complaint, you may file a certification in opposition or a certification in support of a cross complaint which shall not exceed **twenty-five (25)** pages. Any further written responses to the above filed certifications shall not exceed **ten (10)** pages. Forms are available at njcourts.com

Form Promulgated by Directive #08-11 (09/02/2011), CN 11492 (Verified Complaint or Counterclaim - Non-Dissolution Docket)
Kit Revised 07/2012, CN 11492(Non-dissolution "FD" case - How to file a non-divorce application)   page 13 of 17

Again, I heard from my lawyer, telling me your mother was going to sign the order and for me to withdraw my motion. I didn't want to go to court and, being naïve, I adjourned my motion.

SUPERIOR COURT OF NEW JERSEY
CHANCERY DIVISION - FAMILY PART
COUNTY: HUDSON

DWAYNE TAYLOR
_____
Plaintiff

DOCKET NO.: FD - _____

CS NO: _____

vs.

WHITNEY ENGLISH
_____
Defendant

CIVIL ACTION

**Verified Complaint or
Counterclaim**

I, Dwayne Taylor _____ by way of verified complaint/counterclaim, I certify the following:

1. I am the ☑ Plaintiff ☐ Defendant in the above-captioned matter.

2. Plaintiff resides at: Address: 100 South Inman Avenue
   City/Town: Avenel
   County: Middlesex   State: NJ   Zip Code: 07001

   Defendant resides at: Address: Parkside East, 30 Newport Parkway, Apt 2112
   City/Town: Jersey City
   County: Hudson   State: NJ   Zip Code: 07310

3. The child(ren) pertaining to this complaint are:

Name	Date of Birth	M/F	Residing at	Residing with (relationship)
WILLIAM	02/20/2018	M	Parkside East, 30 Newport Parkway, Apt 2112, JC, NJ	Mother

4. Other interested parties' name(s) and address(es):

I have been previously involved in the following family court actions with regard to any of the parties or children listed above. (If yes, give the title of case and docket number.)
☐ Yes   ☐ No

Title of Case (_____ vs. _____)   Docket Number

a. _____

b. _____

c. _____

Form Promulgated by Directive #06-11 (09/02/2011), CN 11492 (Verified Complaint or Counterclaim - Non-Dissolution Docket)
Kit Revised 07/2012, CN 11492(Non-dissolution "FD" case - How to file a non-divorce application)   page 11 of 17

But your mother still did not sign the order. Tired of the games, I was in the process of preparing for court when your mother finally signed the order and had the test done.

Account Information
Account Number: 29739005
NJ Private Account
Acct Ref 1: S1J0611104
Acct Ref 2:
Acct Ref 3:
Trenton, NJ 08519

Laboratory Corporation of America
P.O. Box 2230 Burlington, NC 27216   Telephone: (336) 584-8121   Relationship Report

LabCorp Case #   C0Y-002585

Relationship	Party		Race	Data Collected
Mother	ENGLISH, WHITNEY	86I-1171-0	Black	06/14/2018
Child	ENGLISH, WILLIAM	86I-1172-0		06/14/2018
Alleged Father	TAYLOR, DWAYNE	86K-1026-0	Black	06/18/2018

DNA Analysis

	D3S1358	D7S820	vWA	D12S391	D8S1179	D6S818	D13S317	YH01	TPOX	D2S1338
M	16, 17	9	16, 19	16, 19	13, 15	11	12	8, 7	6, 10	24, 25
C	14, 16	9, 11	16, 16	16, 17	15, 16	11	12	6, 9	8, 10	18, 24
AF	14, 15	10, 11	14, 15	17	12, 16	11, 13	10, 12	8, 9	8, 9	19
PI	5.28	2.40		14.96		8.13	2.17	1.19	3.33	1.49	6.05

DNA Analysis

	D19S433	D22S1045	D2S441	D10S1248	D1S1656	D6S1043	DYS392
M	13, 14	11, 16	10, 11.3	16	12, 14	13, 19	
C	13, 14	15, 16	11.3, 14	11, 16	12, 16	18, 19	11
AF	13, 14	15	11, 14	11, 14	11, 15	17, 18	11
PI	2.11	4.11	1.87	13.45	2.80	7.89	1.37

Conclusion:

Combined Paternity Index: 782,372,509 to 1   Probability of Paternity: 99.99% (Prior Probability = 0.5)

The alleged father, DWAYNE TAYLOR, cannot be excluded as the biological father of the child, WILLIAM ENGLISH, since they share genetic markers. Using the above systems, the probability of paternity is 99.99%, as compared to an untested, unrelated man of the Black population.

I, the undersigned, upon being duly sworn on oath, do depose and state that I read the foregoing report on the analysis of specimens from the above-named individuals, signed by myself, and under penalties for perjury it is my belief that the facts and results therein are true and correct.

Megan D Shaffer, Ph.D.

State of North Carolina
County of Alamance

I, _____ LORI H CRAIG _____, certify that Megan D Shaffer, Ph.D. personally came before me this day and acknowledged that he (or she) is a person authorized by Laboratory Corporation of America Holdings, a corporation, to execute the foregoing on behalf of the corporation.

Subscribed and sworn to (or affirmed) before me this _____ 20 JUN 2018 _____ at Burlington, NC.

Notary Public

LORI H CRAIG
NOTARY PUBLIC
ALAMANCE COUNTY, NC
My Commission Expires 3-1-2020

Laboratory Corporation of America Holdings is accredited by the AABB.

Page 1 of 1

So now it was confirmed 99.9%! I was your father!! Finally!!! At this point, I'm thinking things are confirmed, now we can move on, figure out a parenting scheme and stop wasting time. I was excited thinking I would finally get to see you.

6/21/18, 12:04 PM - Dwayne Taylor: Test results are in. Not that you didnt know but William is my son!

6/21/18, 3:45 PM - Dwayne Taylor: Are we gonna handle this like adults?

6/21/18, 3:46 PM - Dwayne Taylor: I would like to see him and my mother would too

6/22/18, 7:55 AM - Dwayne Taylor: Can we please set up a date and time we can see the baby.

6/23/18, 7:47 AM - Dwayne Taylor: Whitney can we please set up a time I can see him. Please!

7/18/18, 11:33 AM - Dwayne Taylor: Listen... Is there something we do so we can see William? My daughter is going away to school she'd like to see him before she goes. We all would. Doesn't have to be long. Could be a public place. Even if its your mom bringing him in front of your building

7/18/18, 5:07 PM - Dwayne Taylor: We can sit down and text like this. Or talk on the phone about how things should be.

Even after the testing was complete, she still refused to let me, or my side of your family see you. Why?! Put in this position again, I had no choice but to take it to court. But this time it went to trial.

5. A Child Protection Agency (i.e. the Division of Youth and Family Services) (or a similar agency in another State) has been involved with the child(ren) or listed parties.
   ☐ Yes   ☐ No

6. This is an active public assistance case governed by 41 U.S.C.A. 602 (A) (26), N.J.S.A. 44. 10-1.1. et seq.
   ☐ Yes   ☐ No

7. I seek the following for the child(ren) named on page 1:

   ■ Establish Paternity   ☐ Establish Maternity

   ■ Custody
      ■ Joint Legal Custody   ☐ Sole Legal Custody   ☐ Physical Custody

   ☐ Support Order: I am seeking the establishment of a court order against the person who is the spouse/civil union or domestic partner and/or parent of the persons listed on page 1 and has a legal duty to support same pursuant to N.J.S.A. 9:17-38 et seq. Chapter 92. The law requires that child support provisions of court orders shall be enforced by immediate income withholding upon the obligor's current or future income due from an employer or future employer, unemployment compensation or income from any source unless the obligor and obligee agree, in writing to an alternative arrangement or either party demonstrates and the court finds good cause for establishing an alternative arrangement (N.J.S.A. 2A:17-56.9). For the reason(s) checked below, the defendant is under a legal duty to support and maintain the person(s) mentioned on page 1 of this complaint:

      ☐ Plaintiff/Defendant is my lawful wife/husband/domestic partner/civil union partner

      ☐ Plaintiff/Defendant is the biological mother/father of the child(ren) named on page 1

   Reason for seeking custody and/or support:
   _____
   _____
   _____
   _____

   ■ Establish court ordered parenting time arrangements
      ■ Parenting Time   ☐ Grandparent Time   ☐ Sibling Time

   Reasons for requesting court ordered parenting time arrangements:
   Please see Plaintiff's Certification attached hereto
   _____
   _____
   _____

   ☐ Medical Coverage Requested
      ☐ Health Benefits for myself
      ☐ Health Benefits for the child(ren) named in this complaint

All I wanted was to see you and take care of you. I wanted to do my part in raising you. I wanted to have my time with you. I asked the court to grant me joint custody, visitation twice a week, a few holidays, and a time to take you on vacation. That is basically it. I didn't want to take you away from her. I just wanted time with you, my son.

143

In a court hearing both parties get to have a say, basically telling their side of the story. Both parties request things and, through negotiations, the court determines who gets what. In your mother's response, it was quite a different story. Your mother wanted child support, she wanted me to pay her medical bills, your medical bills, her lawyer fees, her transportation fees for going back and forth to visit you in the hospital, and she wanted me to go to anger management classes.

144

I had issues with everything she asked for. How can you ask for child support from the person you said wasn't the father of your child and pushed away after they tried so many times to be there? Why should I be responsible for her medical bills when she had her own insurance? If she had given me the information I needed and put me on your birth certificate, your medical bills would have been paid. Why should I have to pay for her transportation when she always rejected my offers in the past and didn't tell me when she needed a ride to the hospital? All this, after telling me I wasn't your father. Her attempt to make the court send me to anger management was nothing but a spiteful request. She did that because with all that happened I thought she had a mental breakdown and thought she should go to a doctor for an evaluation. She had done so many uncharacteristic things, her behavior led me to believe she was going through something. I had genuine concerns for her mental health and for your safety.

The court attempts to let both parties settle things amongst themselves, this process is called mediation. My role in that was to pick out one of the mediators your mother selected. But she never did that.

7/19/18, 10:37 AM - Dwayne Taylor: Ok... Well. My lawyer says according to papers the ball is in your court to. Pick out 3 mediators. Could you do that so we can handle this please

Although mediation is part of the process before going to trial, I knew it was going to be a waste of time. We never went through the personal mediation, so we went to trial. In trial, the judge scheduled a mediation through the court, which we both had to attend but as expected it was also a waste of time. Mediation is supposed to be between both parties absent of lawyers, however your mother's lawyers were present, and they tried to attend the mediation. That set the tone for the whole trial.

In trial, I again saw a side of your mother I had never seen before. She disobeyed the judge's orders, she lied about things that happened in our relationship, and she tried to make me seem like I was a mean and angry person by taking text out of context. She even said I threatened her and her mother. What surprised me was how she conducted herself, it was unfit for anyone, especially a lawyer. How could she put her hand up and promise to tell the truth and then lie? And why lie? If you thought everything you did was in the best interest of the child, why would you feel the need to lie?

Many months had passed, and court was still going on. We spent almost a year in court for something we could have settled in minutes. The best thing that came from court was that I was able to see you on Saturday's while the trial proceeded. It was unfair that I had to have supervised visits, but at least I got to see you. Unfortunately, I was only able to see you for one hour in a courtroom. The accommodations weren't the best, but we were together.

The only other good thing that happened in court, was that I was able to put my name on documents stating that, if something were to happen to your mom, I was your father and you wouldn't have to go to a temporary foster home; you would come with me.

However, on the last day of court all that came to an end. When the judge gave his ruling, I lost all of that. My name was taken off any documentation associated with you, and I couldn't see you on Saturday's anymore. In my honest opinion, with the exception of seeing you, court was a waste of time and a waste of money. Absolutely nothing was resolved. I was right back at square one.

May of 2019 was the last time I saw you. Since then, I have been trying to work things out with your mom and see you. Every week I give your mom my schedule, with the hope that she will give me a time I can go to a doctor's visit with you or take you to the park. Here are some of the emails I send almost weekly:

Dwayne Taylor <dwaynetaylor943@gmail.com>   Fri, Jul 5, 2019 at 4:40 PM
To: Whitney English <whitneyenglish1@gmail.com>

Whitney

I'm writing to see how William is doing. Also to attempt to work this out with you. I want to be in his life and work on a path that would benefit him.

Dwayne Taylor <dwaynetaylor943@gmail.com>   Sun, Jul 28, 2019 at 5:20 PM
To: Whitney English <whitneyenglish1@gmail.com>

Im available to text or email when ever you become available

Dwayne Taylor <dwaynetaylor943@gmail.com>   Wed, Jul 31, 2019 at 6:13 PM
To: Whitney English <whitneyenglish1@gmail.com>

Hello Whitney hope all is well with all of you

I'm available to talk about William when you are. Just let me know when you are able

Dwayne Taylor <dwaynetaylor943@gmail.com>   Fri, Aug 2, 2019 at 10:45 AM
To: Whitney English <whitneyenglish1@gmail.com>

Hello Whitney hope all is ok with you. Trying to reach out again so we can discuss things concerning William. Let
me know when you can discuss things

Dwayne Taylor <dwaynetaylor943@gmail.com>   Wed, Sep 11, 2019 at 8:53 AM
To: Whitney English <whitneyenglish1@gmail.com>

Whitney I would still like to see William and attend a doctors visit with you. I can meet you at any location at any
time. I am available all day tomorrow (Thursday's Sept 12). Next week I am available any day except Thursday.

Dwayne Taylor <dwaynetaylor943@gmail.com>   Mon, Jun 15, 2020 at 8:16 AM
To: Whitney English <WhitneyEnglish1@gmail.com>

I am still trying to see William. I'm available everyday except Wednesday. Let me know what works for you.
I haven't gotten a response from you in close to a year. I don't know if your not getting the emails I send so when
I text you from now on I will be adding your mother to the text.

Dwayne Taylor <dwaynetaylor943@gmail.com>   Sun, Jun 21, 2020 at 1:58 PM
To: Whitney English <WhitneyEnglish1@gmail.com>

Still trying to see William. I'm available everyday except today and Thursday. Let me know what works for you

Dwayne Taylor <dwaynetaylor943@gmail.com>   Mon, Jun 29, 2020 at 11:44 AM
To: Whitney English <WhitneyEnglish1@gmail.com>

Still trying to see William. I'm available Everyday except Monday and Friday. Let me know what works for you

Dwayne Taylor <dwaynetaylor943@gmail.com>   Sun, Jul 12, 2020 at 8:27 AM
To: Whitney English <WhitneyEnglish1@gmail.com>

Still trying to see William and work this all out. I'm available every day this week. Let me know something.

Dwayne Taylor <dwaynetaylor943@gmail.com>   Sat, Jul 18, 2020 at 4:05 PM
To: Whitney English <whitneyenglish1@gmail.com>

Still trying to see William. Available everyday except Thursday.Let me know something.

In July 2019, I had a phone conversation with your mother for the first time since February of 2018. In that conversation, I finally thought we had reached an agreement on child support and visitation. I agreed to send her money; and, in return, I would be able to see you. I wouldn't bring you to my house right away, but I would go to doctor's appointments and have short visits with you. I was going to send her between $400 - $700 a month, that was what I could afford. I sent your mother the first payment as I said I would, and she did not hold up her part of the agreement. She did not let me see you. That was over a year ago.

Whitney English
Payment to $EnglishWhitney

$250.00

Sep 3, 2019 at 1:52 PM

I refuse to send any more money when I couldn't see you. To be honest, I don't know anything about you. I don't know what you look like right now. I hate to say it, but I don't even know if you are alive right now! I feel you are though, I don't believe God would put all this in my heart if you weren't. I'm sorry this is happening to you. I'm sorry you are caught in the middle of this. Right now the only good thing is you are too young to understand what is happening.

I don't know how things got here. I really don't understand why all this happened and why it continues to this day. You are my son and I want to raise you. I want to experience things with you, and watch you grow and explore the world. I want to sit in the stands and watch you play a sport. I want to go to your school play. I am not giving up hope that I will be able to do these things with you. I will not give up on you. I will continue to do what I have to do in order to see you. I will send your mother text messages and emails until I see you!

My goal here, William, is not to make your mother look bad, however she should be held accountable for her actions. The things that she has done and continues to do are not logical and it is unfair to you and me. She is creating this space between you and me. I would love nothing more than to have a relationship with you. I simply want you to know the truth about what has happened. I constantly think of ways to convince your mother into letting me be with you. But I cannot think of anything else besides what I have tried. I'm sorry but I cannot and will not pay all of your mother's bills in order to see you. Most of these bills wouldn't exist if she had just let things take their natural course as I have explained. One day you will ask where I am. Perhaps your mother will tell you that I am a deadbeat, and I don't want you. But that is not true. I would not have done all I have done and continue to do if I didn't want to take care of you. I am not a deadbeat! I do want you! I do want to take care of you! I do love you! And I will not give up on you until God takes my health or takes me off this earth!

WOMEN

This is probably going to be my favorite section of this book. I love talking about the ladies! And "the ladies" love talking about your dad. Some of the things they say are good, however most are probably bad. Because you are my son, the ladies are going to love you! I feel "the ladies", is a significant subject that a father should discuss with his son. Not saying there aren't other important things to talk about like finances and being a good person, which I will talk about later in this book. But "the ladies" is something you must know, as a man! This section is meant for mature eyes so forgive me in advance if you read this book at a young age. I am going to talk to you like the men in my life talked to me. Frankly, this is how men are supposed to talk! Man to Man, no filter! Raw! This section is primarily meant for men. "Barbershop talk". So ladies, if you are reading this, please forgive me in advance for the foul language. The end of this section is sexually explicit and goes into detail. Viewer/reader discretion advised. These comments are my own and don't reflect how every man feels.

I'm just going to put things out how I'm thinking of them. There is no order of importance. I feel everything has its own importance. Remember this is how I feel, mostly my experiences and what I think has worked for me. Some of these things have been passed down to me from the men I looked up to as a youngster.

- Getting the girl

- Always respect the women in your life.

- Women can be very insecure at times. You have to give her that assurance.

- Treat your lady how you want to be treated.

- Buy your girlfriend flowers and random gifts, occasionally.

- Learn to understand your woman.

- Women are never wrong.

- No romance without finance.

- Women have a hard time making decisions.

- Some women are emotional. Understand emotion has no logic.

-Don't let women drive you crazy.

- Don't hit a lady…unless that woman hits you. At this point, she is no longer a lady she is an enemy.

-Don't put any woman on a pedestal. They are human beings just like you.

- Don't ever think you are special! The bad or foul thing that a woman did to the man before you she will do to you.

- Always save something for yourself.

- Don't ever expose other people's secrets.

- Keep things that happen between you and a woman, between the two of you.

- Some women are absolutely Crazy and out of their minds!

- Women want your full undivided attention... ALWAYS. When your woman is talking, listen to her.

- When having emotional conversations, be careful what you say because women believe things you say.

- Women want you to listen to them. They don't want you to try to fix the problem they just want to vent about it.... FOREVER

- Never let a woman talk you into anything you know is wrong.

- Don't ever marry a woman before you live with her.

- Women ask for the truth but they don't really want it!

- If a woman wants to see you after 10:00 at night, go!

- If a woman pulls her titties out, suck them!

- Getting the booty

- Always have a separate or hidden bank account.

- If she wants to leave, let her leave.

-What to do if you get a woman pregnant?

-Some women don't need to be in your life.

There are many ways you can go about approaching a girl.
The best and easiest way I find is simply walking up to her,
looking her in her eyes, and saying hello. Give her the
reason you approached her. You can say, "Hello my name
is William. I saw you come in the room, I think you are
beautiful, and I would like to get to know you better if I
can." Now before you do any of that, make sure you are
looking good. You must have a nice haircut, must be
dressed nice, and your breath must smell good. A tic-tac
will do or a small breath mint, you can have chewing gum
because it last longer, but don't chew the gum while talking
to her. Never be afraid to approach this woman, even if she
is the best-looking woman in the room and you are a little
nervous. You may get rejected by this woman, don't take it
personally. She may not be interested, for whatever reason.
You will get rejected by more women than accepted. When
your offer is rejected, no worries, her loss. Just say, "Oh
okay no problem, you were worth a chance. Have a good
day," (or evening, which ever applies). Rejection sucks and
looks bad in front of your boys but, at times, you have to
take a chance, no guts no glory. As I said not all women are
going to reject you; and, when you get the fine woman that

everyone was too intimidated to talk to, it will all be worth it. Buy her a drink, have a quick conversation, get the cell number, and ask her if she would rather chill with her girls or you. Give her the option. She may want to chill with the peeps she came with, but if the conversation you are having with her is good, she may want to talk to you more. Still, if she wants to chill with her peeps, cool. You got the number, call her the next day and invite her out to coffee or for another drink where you met.

Women are a beautiful gift from God. True companionship with a woman is one of the best things in this world. It is something you should respect. It is something you should cherish. Our black women have a very hard time in this world. They don't get treated well by many other races and sometimes not even by our own race. It is ironic that our women are treated so badly sometimes yet are one of the most imitated in this world. Sassiness, independence, that pretty bronze skin which other races get tans to obtain, are all traits of our black women. Because of this, when she comes to you, give her that respect she needs. Show her the love that the rest of the world won't. She needs that from you. Now, if you choose to date a woman out of your race that is fine. She still needs that respect, love, and comfort from you that the world sometimes does not offer.

Tell your woman how beautiful she is often; woman need to hear that from you. When you are in a relationship with a woman, you are a very important person to her. She will open up to you and be vulnerable. You have to let her know how important she is to you as well. Let her know there is no woman more important to you than her. Kiss her randomly on the forehead and on the cheek, give her a hug for no reason, call her or text her just to say hello or to tell her you were thinking of her.

Treat your lady how you want to be treated. If you want love, you have to show love. If you want trust, you have to trust her. If you want forgiveness, you must forgive her. There is nothing you can ask for from a woman that you are not willing to give her.

On special days like her birthday, Christmas, and anniversaries buy her something nice. Put some thought in it! These days don't change. Do not let life make you forget these days. Make a plan for these days and try not to buy the same stuff over and over again, unless she likes that kind of thing. Start planning out a month in advance just in case you want to take her on a trip. Oh, and every trip you go on, have some roses waiting in the room with wine, if you can. On random days, buy her something small like flowers or her favorite candy or snack. Take her out to a movie or dinner on a weekday, don't always wait for the weekend.

One critical thing you must do is learn about your woman. If you want to be a good boyfriend/husband, pay attention to your woman. It's not always going to be what she says but her reaction to things. Understand what upsets her and avoid that if you can. Understand what she likes, looking at her body language and facial expressions. Women cannot hide either of those. If you really pay attention, those two things will tell you everything. If you see her constantly looking at something online that might be the one thing she wants. If you walk past that one store in the mall and she keeps looking at that purse, she may want it. Pay attention to what she says too, you will pick up a lot of information that way. You will learn quickly what she doesn't like sooner than you will learn what she likes because some women need to vent! Listen to her when she vents! Now, on those occasions when you get the complaint, the mean facial expression, and the bad body language, stay away from that shit son!!! That is the "Trifecta"! Whatever they are complaining about, DO NOT DO IT! Avoid it, if humanly possible.

Don't ever expect an apology. Cause you ain't gonna get it. Some women are never wrong. In their world, they are always right. Even when they contradict themselves in the same sentence, they are always right. Don't fight this; avoid the argument and accept it. Even when it's proven she is wrong, she will still be convinced she is right. However, this only applies to little unimportant stuff. Like what she said yesterday about something you said. If deep down you know your right about something, go with what you think.

Before you think about getting in a serious relationship, make sure you have a job son. You will not be able to do many things if you have no money. You can't take her out or buy anything nice for her, if you have no money. You are way more attractive to a woman, and she will be more open to your advances, if she sees you are responsible, independent and have a few dollars in your pocket. To be bluntly honest, without these things you ain't getting no booty, from a smart woman anyway.

Some women have a hard time making decisions. To this day, I could be hanging out with a girl and say to her, "Hey let's go to McDonalds," and she could say, "Okay, I haven't had that in a while." Now, the menu at McDonalds has not changed for years! You figure when you suggest a place to eat and she accepts the restaurant that she would start thinking about what she wants to eat. But when you pull up in the drive-thru and turn to her and say, "What would you like?"; she says, "Give me a second." Then that second becomes minutes and the person asking begins to get annoyed and cars start piling up behind you, you begin to wonder what is she thinking about? Then you ask her "Is everything alright?" and she will say, "Yes I just don't know what I want." Don't get upset here son. Even though she's going to put you through all of that just to get the same damn thing she always gets! They sometimes put too much thought into very simple things. Ironic thing is they will tell us we don't put enough thought into things. Some women are very complex, you will learn that.

Some women are emotional on a level you will never understand. They make decisions the, because of these emotions, will leave you dumbfounded. One day she will eventually make a choice about something, let's say for example, the way the furniture is arranged in your house. She will be very particular about the placement of everything in the room, even the arrangement of pillows on the couch. If you come along and move something, she's going to fix it back to the way she had it and share with you her not very nice thoughts about the crime you just committed. Then you are going to come home three days later, and all the furniture is going to be rearranged because of how she was feeling. Now the pillows can be arranged the way you did it the other day. You better not put it back the old way she wanted it!

Women are very complex. Having said this (and I will again later I'm sure), do not let these women drive you crazy. This is just a small example, they will say something and then when you do what they asked, they are going to say, "I didn't ask you to do that." You are going to be certain they did, while they will be certain they did not. Your mother was infamous for this! We would talk about something and she would be steadfast on her position. Then the next day, she would say the exact opposite and stand firmly behind that.

One of the most important things to remember is: Never hit a lady! Like I said, they are going to attempt to drive you crazy, so no matter what, do not put your hands on a woman. That is a place you do not want to be. Our role, as men, is to protect our women, not hit them or hurt them. Learn how to control your emotions now. If you feel like you are going to hit a woman, walk away. Go somewhere to cool yourself down. If you hit your wife or girlfriend, you are going to change that relationship forever, not to mention run the risk of getting arrested. If you have children around, that will make a bad situation even worse. Find other ways to deal with stressful situations before hitting your lady. If you feel that you always want to hit this woman, then this is not the woman for you. Some would say to go to counseling, I'm saying get another woman, unless you have a family with her. In that case, you have to do all you can to try to make it work. However, if a woman hits you, you gotta defend yourself! You shouldn't put your hands on her, and she shouldn't put her hands on you. Some women will try to hurt you because you hurt them. Some take things too far, attempting to hurt you permanently for example using a deadly weapon. At this point, she is no longer a woman; she is an enemy, and enemies have no gender.

You can love a woman deeply and you should! The right one deserves all of your love. However, don't love a woman more than you love yourself. Don't put your woman on a pedestal. You shouldn't look up to any woman except your mother and grandmother. Many men make this mistake. They put their women before themselves all the time. Putting a woman's needs before yours some of the time is okay, but not all the time. You are important too. Your needs are just as important or sometimes more important than hers. You are equal.

That bad or foul thing she did to her ex-lover for whatever reason, she may do to you. If she cheated on him with you, there is a good chance she will cheat on you with the next man. Don't ever let a woman sweet talk you into thinking you are the best thing that happened to them. To some degree, at the beginning of the relationship you might be. Everything is beautiful at the beginning of a relationship. But the harder she falls in love, when something happens that she doesn't like, or you do something that her ex did; the worse your punishment is going to be. You are only special when things are going in a direction she likes. When things start calming down or going in a way she doesn't like, you will not be that "best thing" anymore.

162

This does not apply to all women. This has been one of my experiences. I am just giving you a heads up.

Finding a woman to fall in love with and becoming vulnerable is the world God intended for us. It is *thee* most beautiful thing on this earth. You will want to show her all of who you are. You will want to expose all of yourself to her. The more you think you expose, the better you think the relationship will be. But here is where you have to careful. You give all of yourself, every ounce of love in you, then suddenly that disagreement happens, that horrible argument that will one day happen. Then all the personal things you shared of yourself are being thrown back in your face and possibly exposed to potentially anyone and everyone. All that love you gave was for nothing. Don't let this happen to you. Understand, you have to risk exposing yourself to experience that feeling, but not so much that it costs you your individuality and sanity. I said all that to say always keep something inside for yourself. Don't give everything for anyone. Keep some for you.

Do not expose to this woman, or anyone for that matter, secrets that have been entrusted to you by others, because a scorned woman can expose that. If a person trusts you enough to tell you something of themselves that is personal and damaging, you must keep it to yourself forever! You might one day be the person telling the secret that you want protected.

Things that happen between you and a woman, good or bad, stays between the two of you. Don't share with anyone the reasons for the small argument you had. Don't go online into a group discussion exposing a mistake she made. It is not everyone's concern what you and your lady are disagreeing about. On the other side of that, don't go sharing with everyone the great things either. You might not want to let some people know how good your girl is in bed, they might try to see for themselves one day. When a woman knows she can trust you, she will become more open and relaxed around you. But if you mishandle that trust even once she will always put up a wall around you. That "wall" is the beginning of the end for that relationship.

Son, please understand some women are crazy! No matter what you do or what you say, they are going to remain crazy. The problem with the crazy ones in my experience, is that they are usually the most loyal. You sometimes don't find out until it's too late though. These are usually the ones who stalk you and call 20 times, leaving messages. So, when you're walking around and you feel someone is watching you, look in the bushes and in the parked cars. Most are probably just misunderstood and have had experiences that made them this way. Either way, you might not want to get involved with them. You will see little signs like those mentioned above and other things like people saying, "Yea she crazy, be careful dude." Women that smile a lot or stare in the air a lot with weird facial expressions are suspect too in my experience. And watch out for her parents if they're being a little too nice and welcoming. Her father especially, should look you up and down a few times and give you the speech about how much he loves his daughter and show you the "gun". If you don't get the "What are your intentions with my daughter" speech and they love you the first time they meet you, get the hell out of there, son! Cause she crazy! Don't ignore those red flags and that gut feeling when associating with one. Look for the signs, son! I was attempting to be comical here but serious at the same time. Just be careful who you let in your life.

When your woman is talking to you, she thinks she is '*thee*' most important thing to you and expects you to give her your undivided attention. You could be in the middle of open-heart surgery, she does not care! She expects you to stop whatever you are doing and pay attention. She has a lot of things to say about her day and she does not want you to miss anything. She does not want you to make her repeat herself, she will do that when she wants to, and she will do it numerous times. So, stop what you are doing because she is going to tell you everything that happened from the time she woke up that morning until the second before she entered the room you are currently in. Son, this includes everything! What others said, what other people wore and there will be a test after in the form of questions like, "What do you think of that?" or "What would you have done in that situation, William?" So pay attention.

Be careful and mindful of things you say to your lady, good and bad, because they believe the things you say to them. I've made the mistake of promising things to women and then not fulfilling those promises. Doing that takes away your creditability until you can fulfill the promise, be aware though that some promises have time limits. More important than that, in the middle of a heated argument, do not say something in that argument you are going to regret. Don't throw in her face something she entrusted you with. They will not forget it. They know you did that just to hurt them. Don't ever intentionally try to hurt your lady. That is the beginning of the end for the relationship.

As a man, when we are confronted with a problem or something that concerns us, we try to fix it. When women approach you to talk, they sometimes just want to vent. They don't want you to try to fix the problem or give them advice, they just want you to listen and nod your head 'yes' with as little feedback as possible. They simply want you to understand, from their perspective, why there is a problem. I'm telling you now you are not going to understand in most instances. But fight the urge to fix the problem or offer advice son because that is not what they want. If they don't ask your opinion, don't give it. Give advice when they ask.

Some women constantly try to test you. They want to see how far you would go and what you would do for them. Do not do something you know is wrong for a woman. These types of women will use their bodies and words to manipulate you. Do not fall victim to this. Wars in this world have started over women doing this. So many men are in jail today over something a woman persuaded them to do. While that man is rotting in jail that woman moved on to the next man doing the same thing. If it's wrong, don't do it.

Don't ever marry a woman before really getting to know her. Unfortunately, sometimes you never really know a person, it's either that or people go through so many changes. One minute they are one way and the next they are someone else. I've known people to act like my best friend one day and act as if they don't know me the next.

166

They will walk right past you and not say a word. I'm getting off topic though. Don't marry a woman before you live with her. I have seen 10-year relationships end in two weeks after people have moved in together. Imagine being with that person for 10 years and getting married just to have it annulled? Before you get your heart into a relationship too deep, learn how this person lives, learn their habits and lifestyle. When you're dating this person, it's easy for them to hide who they really are. But if you are in their private space, it's more difficult to hide certain habits. For example, if they are a slob you will see it as soon as you walk into their house. The place is going to be a mess, there will be a sink full of dishes with bugs flying around the dishes, and so on. This may be an issue for you. This could potentially be a deal breaker. Early discovery of certain issues will save you a lot of heartache later. So get to know that woman and as many bad habits as you can. After learning her habits and she learns yours, if you still find each other attractive, move in together. Now you have to see how your lifestyles and all those bad habits mix. One day, an issue is going to come up. You have to see how both of you are going to handle it. It's much easier to go your separate ways without being married if the problem is serious. Understand though, in a serious relationship, problems are going to come up every so often, therefore don't give up easily. However, some problems cannot be swept under the rug, especially those repeated ones. Don't let a woman or anyone constantly disrespect you, always stand up for yourself. Piggybacking off of that, don't marry her without testing out the bedroom activities, or as the saying goes "never buy a car without test driving it first."

Sex is a very important part of a relationship, but more on that later.

Some women ask for the truth, son, but they really don't want it. Most of the time, they already know the truth. They just want you to make them feel a different way about it. For example, if your woman approaches you and asks if she looks fat in her dress, your response is always no! She knows she looks fat in that dress, she wants you to convince her that she doesn't. Now be smart, give your honest opinion for serious things. If she has a heart disease and asks you if she should eat that bucket of fried chicken, you gotta say no to that. However, "Am I fat in this dress?" IS ALWAYS A NO.

If you are dating and that woman calls you after 10:00 pm at night and invites you over to watch a movie, you go! She doesn't really want to watch the movie, son, what she really wants is "The Dick"! See she is trying to be lady-like, she can't come out and say she wants sex at that stage in the relationship. Now, later on, when you had a few sessions and she gets a little more familiar with you she may come out and say that, but not now. It is important that you do a few things after accepting the invitation. First off, take a shower and powder your balls. Make sure you smell good all over and that you are clean, especially make sure your breath is good. Next, never go over her house empty handed. Take a bottle of red wine. Red wine makes them feel sexy son! Next, take 2 forms protection with you, always have 3 or more condoms with you. Be prepared for multiple rounds and also breakages. The other form of protection is a knife or something to protect yourself. Some

168

women love drama, and some are out to get you. As I mentioned before some women are crazy and some have other intentions like to rob you or even hurt you. Unfortunately, in the world we live in, you have to be prepared for just about anything. They will lure you in with sex to take advantage of you. There are many women in this world like this, stay alert and be careful. But if you get the one that truly wants "The Dick", have fun. There are many in the world like this too!

As my great Uncle Cleveland use to say, "If your woman pulls out her titties in front of you, suck them!" Women love sex just as much as we do, son. If your woman wants to have sex, give it to her! The more she trusts you and is comfortable around you, the more sex you will have with her. Sex is a very important part of a relationship. Sex alone can be the reason relationships end. Either lack of sex in the relationship or one person is having sex outside of the relationship. You have to be open and honest about your sexual expectations. That is one area that both partners should be perfectly honest about. There will be times that the two of you aren't on the same page sexually. Most of the time, it's going to be you wanting it and her not. Try not to step out of the relationship if this happens. I had issues with this in relationships, I stepped out. It did cause problems and the relationship ended. I learned later that if I had just talked to her about what I was feeling, we may have been able to work things out. If you run into this problem, talk to her about it. You may be pleasantly surprised with the outcome.

Alright here it is, you wined her, and you dined her, she's open. You got the booty call, it's safe. Now when you go inside and she is in there with nothing but a robe on, fresh out the shower, this is 100% booty call. This is the situation you want to be in! This woman wants "The Dick". But you still have to be chill, calm, and precise. Always start with a kiss on the cheek, which you do as soon as you get there while handing her the bottle of wine. Now when she goes to pour the wine, this is your final time to check and make sure you are good. Make sure your breath is good, make sure you got your condoms, and do a final body check (arm pits and balls check). Also say your grace cause you about to eat this woman up! You can and should do these checks just before going inside but you may be a little nervous and forget, plus she might be looking out for you in the window. As she brings the wine in the room, you stand up when she enters the room. Help her by taking the glasses of wine so she can sit down and get comfortable. As you sip the wine, and she picks the movie, tell her she smells good and move in a little closer. Give her another kiss on the cheek, move slowly while you gauge what she wants and the speed she wants to go by her movements. If, after the cheek kiss, she grabs the wine again then you have to wait a while and let her loosen up with more wine. However, if you give her the cheek kiss and she turns her head to kiss you on the mouth, then you can proceed because she is ready to go. Kiss her deeply and softly at first, she will let you know the tempo by her body movement and breathing. When women get turned on their breathing gets rapid and heavy. But the best indicator and a sexy one is their nipples get hard. This is when you start touching her body, start

170

with upper, outer thighs, waist, and back. The kissing should get more passionate at this point, this is when you move down and start kissing and periodically, gently licking her neck. This is all done slowly, don't rush any of this, take your time son. While kissing the neck you should also start undoing her robe to start disrobing all that beauty. Now, if you do this right, she should start to disrobe you too, depending on the lady. Now you want to move down to the titties. Son be very sensitive here, always take your time with the titties! Don't just focus on the nipple but the whole breast, massage and gently suck. Let her moans and movements dictate your actions. Keep in mind though, not all women like a lot of breast attention, again use her movements to let you know. If she's not all that into the breast attention, move on. Your hands should get familiar with every inch of her body, from head to toe. If she is a woman that knows what she wants and what she's doing, she knows how to kiss and touch you. The mood should be hot at this point and you should have fully explored her body. Now it's time for your kisses to move even lower to the stomach and the inner thighs. Take your time here, you want to move slowly and tease her a little with the oral sex. Be aware performing oral sex on a woman does not guarantee she will return the favor. There are many ways to "go down" on a woman. Some say write out the woman's name with your tongue. I say work around the whole area, women like different things. Some like slow soft long strokes, while others like hard quick strokes for example. Try a few different things and, when she lets out that loud moan, grabs the back of your head with both hands, squeezes your head with her thighs, starts doing the pelvis thrust and shouting, "Don't stop;" you found what works for that woman son; good job! If she is a woman that wants to please you, she will return the favor. This works basically the same way, let her find out what works on you. Only difference is unlike her, you can't orgasm here. Women have the God-given ability to be able to orgasm multiple times in one session, most men cannot. You have to calm things down within yourself so you can now give her "The Dick". Some women don't always want to have an orgasm from oral sex, some want it through intercourse, and the smart ones want both. At some point, usually while you are going down on her, you have to get the condom ready. Once you get into the sex flow you really don't want to stop so turn off your phone in advance or anything else that could interrupt things. When the condom is on, son its time to go to work. Entry is the magical moment and should be prolonged. Take your time here and, when you go in, go in deep; leave it in; and let it marinate for about 10-15 seconds before you start stroking. Start off slowly, it's like the warm-up before the workout, then gradually build your speed and impact of your thrust but take your time doing this. Then, after a while, it's time to turn it up! It's time to air her out and get rid of all your frustrations. It is time to fling her around like a doll. Turn her around, slap her ass, and pull her hair. Put her legs on your shoulders and get in there, by the time you're done you should have the best stomach work out ever. Take that woman like it's the last time you will ever have sex. When you are done, that woman's legs should still be trembling while she lays on your chest. Before you leave, you should dispose of your condom by pouring the remains in the toilet before or after urinating, and then rinse out the condom before putting it in the trash. When you get home wash up good before calling her or texting her, thanking her for a nice evening. That early morning and the rest of the day, it's going to be on your mind. Do not start stalking the woman or keep calling her, only talk about it if she brings it up. You can compliment her on it, but don't dwell on it.

Some women love to spend money! They especially love it when it's not their own. Don't ever give a woman access to all of your money and credit. Even when things are going well, she will take all of your money. She will use your money for the bills and save all of hers. If she has a good job, she can pay some of the bills she helps create. When things are bad though, she will take every dime you have and run your credit up to the limit, sometimes buying stuff for another dude. You can have a joint bank account but never put all your money in it. Never have your whole paycheck from your job directly deposited into this joint bank account. Always have at least two bank accounts no one knows about except you. You must be able to take care of yourself. Don't allow any woman to take everything away from you.

If a woman decides she doesn't want to be with you anymore, let her go. Don't throw yourself in front of the door or change into something she wants you to be. Always remember who you are. Don't allow a person to change you, forgetting who you are. Some will change you for the hell of it and still leave you. Some relationships have time limits and some simply don't last. Don't fight for something that she is not willing to fight for. I did this with your mother, I almost lost who I was. I was willing to do almost anything to be with her, but she didn't want it. It hurt me and I was lost. I was fortunate enough to have people in my life to help me find myself again. This is what I want for you. I want to be able to talk to you when you have a difficult time. I want to be there to help you through things you think are too big for you. I want to be your father.

What should you do if you should get a woman pregnant? The woman you choose should be a woman you trust and love, a woman that is very special to you because she is going to be in your life forever! You might want to wait until you are married to have children, but sometimes emotions take over and that may not happen for you. Please understand that woman has the final say on what happens during that pregnancy. What I mean is she determines if a baby is going to be born or not. There are going to be good days and bad days during this pregnancy, so prepare yourself. She is going to be sweet one minute and sour the next. She will be mean one minute and sensitive the next. It may be an emotional rollercoaster, but she will one day go back to normal. As much as you love and trust this woman, when that baby is born, get a DNA test. You have to be sure that child is yours before you get deeply emotionally connected.

Some women do not need to be in your life. Some of the women you meet are going to be trash and they aren't going to add anything positive to your life. They are just around to take whatever they can from you. Most of the time, all they really want is your money. They come with the sob stories or the damsel in distress routine. Try to avoid these women. They appear to be nice at first, but then time goes by and that sweet facade goes away and you notice you only see them on two occasions - when they are broke and when you get paid. They always seem to know when you get paid. When they see you picked up on their game, they start offering sex. If you think you are the only person they are offering sex to, then read this chapter all over again! Stay away from them! Some people are pieces of shit son, that's the bottom line.

These are my experiences and some from relatives and friends. You may go through something that is totally different. You may have relationships with women that are all good, it's possible. I do know some men that have wives, and they get along very well, some never have arguments. I find that hard to believe, but who am I to say it isn't true.

My intentions here were not to scare you, but to make you aware of what is out in this world. Just to be clear, it is not always the goal to get in a woman's pants. I am merely saying that if you are making love to your woman often, that suggests you are both happy and satisfied, and you are expressing that love and happiness to each other. It is a good gauge to see how things are going. Relationships are a wonderful thing, and something you need in your life. I feel men need women just as much as women need men. We don't need each other for financial reasons, each party should be independent in many areas of life. We need each other for companionship and to start and raise a family. There are things in this world that only a woman can give a man and vice versa. That is why God made it that way. Read Genesis in the Bible about Adam and Eve. Life with the right woman in it can be amazing and fulfilling.

When you find that woman of your dreams, love her deeply. There are challenges with everything in life, relationships are no exception and at times are going to be the biggest challenge in your life. But a woman can help you experience some of the most beautiful things in life such as love and the birth of children. Love is a complicated thing, at times, because people have different interpretations of what it is. When you find out how your woman defines love and you can fulfill it, you will make her a very happy woman and hopefully she will try to do the same for you.

LIFE

This section will probably be another difficult one to write about. I am going to break this section down into two parts. One part, I will talk about being a black man in America. The other part, I will talk about life in general, basically how you live life, rules to live by, or lessons I want you to know.

There is so much going on in the world right now. As I write you, there is a scary virus going on right now called "Covid-19". This virus is killing people in days! It is believed to have started in Wuhan, China. Scientists think that it originated in a bat. There are others who believe it was made in a lab. There are so many different opinions about this virus that you really don't know which to believe. It supposedly started in late November, early December of 2019. Then, it made its way over to the United States in January or February of 2020. I personally think the virus was here sooner. I recall talking to people who had the same symptoms as those associated with the virus as early as December. As of right now, we have lost approximately 210,000 people to this virus, and the count is expected to go up drastically. The loss of lives, in my opinion, falls on the hands of our president at this time, Donald Trump. He is the leader of this country and he could have taken this virus more seriously than he did and done something to spare so many lives. I think he is one of the worst presidents of our time. I don't believe he is fit for office nor do I think he really knows what he is doing. The thing I dislike most about him is how people reacted to him. I personally think he is a racist and, from what I see, so do a lot of other people. In my opinion, a lot of racist and white supremacists think Trump is on their side. Trump became president in January of 2017. In August of 2017, there was a white supremacy March in Virginia on mainstream television. The thing that was different about this was that no one hid his or her face. Normally, when there is a march like this, people hide their faces with masks. But now they felt they didn't have to. Fortunately, they were met with a lot of resistance and lost momentum. Trump's big slogan was "Make America Great Again." Make America great again for who? There was never a time in the country where America was great for black people.

While this virus is going on, there is an inept president in office, and there was another black man, named George Floyd, who was killed by police. A police officer knelt on George's neck for 8 minutes and 46 seconds while he was handcuffed on the ground. This virus we are experiencing is new, however brutality by police and evil people is not. In fact, brutality and unjust treatment of our people has been going on in this country for centuries and continues today.

In talking about the brutality and unjust treatment of our people in this country, I have to start with transatlantic slave trade, which is believed to have started in 1619. The passage was from Angola, Africa to Virginia. It is believed from 1619-1800 there were over 4 million African slaves in America. There were many forms of slavery in the world. It started almost at the beginning of time and no race has been excluded from it. In fact, at one time in this world there were more white slaves than there were black. Common slavery back then was similar to prison today. You worked off your debt or your time for a crime and you were freed. The reason slavery started in this country is because there was a lot of strenuously hard work to do and no one wanted to do it or could do it all. In most cases, it required working outdoors in high temperatures either in a field or building structures. They didn't have all the fancy machines we have today, most work had to be done by hand. When America was colonized, the Native Americans were made slaves. However, because it was their home, they knew the land and were able to escape. There was also something known as "indentured servants", a person would sign a contract or make a deal stating how long they would work for someone. When that time was done, the servants were free. When the servants' debt was paid, the landowners still needed work to be done in their fields. So something had to be done to fix the problem. Slaves escaping and servants being freed after time served had landowners losing a lot of money, for this reason Europeans sought slaves from Africa.

Even though a person was a slave or indentured servant, they were still treated like a human being in most cases. But the treatment Africans received from the Europeans was horrible. It wasn't the common slavery the world knew, it was a new brutal slavery called "chattel Slavery". Africans were kidnapped from their homes, brought to America, crammed into boats like chained animals and forced to be slaves forever! Even their children were born into slavery and expected to be slaves forever. They had no rights and were considered property for the rest of their lives. They were sold for whatever their masters thought they were worth and separated from their families whenever the master felt like doing so. There was never to be an end. No time served, no debt paid; this was supposed to last forever, and this was the law. There were also other laws, for example, forbidding slaves to learn how to read or write, they weren't allowed to congregate nor were they allowed to vote. This was designed to keep our race down forever.

Please understand the expectations son. FOREVER! This was designed to last forever. At times, you are going to see and hear how the positive laws created in this country to make things better for people were never intended for us. In 1971, A woman by the name of Barbara Jordan said these words at an impeachment hearing for our then President Richard Nixon.

"Earlier today, we heard the beginning of the Preamble to the constitution of the United States. 'We the people.' It's a very eloquent beginning. But when that document was completed on the seventeenth of September 1787 I was not included in that 'We the people'. I felt somehow for many years that George Washington and Alexander Hamilton just left me out by mistake."

But all the negative laws created to keep people down were made only for us. Black people could not have nor keep anything. Women didn't even own the babies that came out of their bodies. The reason black people today don't have a lot, is because we were never supposed to.

African slaves never accepted this, many tried to run away or escape. But remember they didn't know the land, so they were eventually caught and returned to their owner. This is why the Europeans picked them. When the runaway slave was returned, they were punished. Punishments were brutal, they were beaten with whips, had their Achilles cut so they couldn't run anymore or had contraptions placed on them so they couldn't get away without injury. Despite this, some still tried to escape. When they were caught again, they were killed. They were tortured, dragged by horses, even dismembered. The real sickening part about our people being dismembered is the sadistic owners would keep the body part as a souvenir. Even passing it down through generations. But the most famous and popular way to kill back then was lynching or hanging. This was an event people actually came out to see and celebrate. This was also a way to display what would happen to slaves if they got out of line. History would have us believe lynching started with slavery. When you open a book or go on the internet and research lynching, the first picture you see is a black person hanging from a tree. However, there was a time in history when there were more white people lynched than black. This was just how people sought justice then. This went on for hundreds of years.

At the end of slavery, there came about more laws known as the "Jim Crow laws". These laws were put in place to do nothing but keep our race down.

If that wasn't harsh enough, at the end of slavery when one acquired property, most likely from his master that passed away and had no one to leave it to, the former slave couldn't leave it to his family when he passed away. The property went back to the city (something similar to this is still happening today). Son, I advise you to read about our history and learn how our people were treated. Read it from a good source, what I mean is a black source because there have been so many times people from outside the race have mixed up facts and put things out in the world that aren't true. When you read about many black people in certain books, we appear to be weak or uneducated. This again couldn't be further from the truth. There are so many strong, courageous, and admirable black people in our past, you just have to read and find out about them. People such as Harriet Tubman, who I reference a lot because I deeply admire her for many of her achievements. James Baldwin who was a great author and activist. Peter Salem, a slave who fought in the Revolutionary war for his freedom and became a war hero. At a point in the battle of Bunker Hill, the American soldiers were running out of ammo, when the British began to charge them. Peter stood up, shot, and killed the Major of those charging soldiers. But if you look at the artwork of that time, it shows Peter cowering behind the Major who was ready to retreat.

James Armistead was another slave who became a war hero. He was a double spy giving the British bad info and giving the continental army information that some say helped America win the war. Prince Whipple is another slave and war hero who fought with George Washington. He is recognized as one of the men who helped in the early stages of ending slavery. Wentworth Cheswell was another influential figure during the Revolutionary war who rode south while Paul Revere rode west warning the troops that the British were approaching. But if you read most history books they never mention him, only Paul Revere. Fredrick Douglas, George Washington Carver, Jesse Jackson, Martin Luther King, Colin Powell, Jackie Robinson, W.E.B Dubois Sojourner Truth, John Brown, Malcolm X, Madam CJ Walker, Barack Obama and Booker T. Washington just to name a few more worth researching. There are and were so many great black people in the world I can't describe them all. You have to read and see the great things they have done. Learn from our people son, so you can learn what you are capable of achieving.

In this country, no matter what you do, there are some people who do not want to see you succeed. They do not want to accept you as an equal man, even today. After slavery and the adoption of the Jim Crow laws or "Black Code" our people had a hard time finding a way to live. As a result of this, in 1906 a black man by the name of Ottowa W. Gurley bought many acres of land in Tulsa, Oklahoma and created an all-black community later called "The Black Wall Street". This was, even by today's standards, a very lucrative and prosperous area for black people in America. There were over 600 businesses including restaurants, hotels, and every type of store imaginable. There were schools and even a hospital. There were multiple millionaires that owned airplanes, and all these people were black. On May 31, 1921 all of this came to an end when a mob came and destroyed the whole town killing 300 people. This all allegedly happened when a black man was accused of assaulting a white woman in an elevator. The white lady named Sarah Page did not want to prosecute, claiming he did not attack her and that he had slipped and bumped into her. But the mob claimed an eyewitness saw him attack her and they wanted him lynched. Some men from the town where the young black man lived came to support him and that raised tension at the courthouse resulting in a couple of people getting killed, which started the "Tulsa Massacre". This was just an excuse for the mob to burn down and loot this thriving black town continuing to keep another race down. Black Wall Street was worth Millions. Not one person was ever prosecuted.

This wasn't the first nor last time there has been a black massacre like this. The Colfax Louisiana Massacre of 1873 happened because there was going to be a shift of power favoring black people. Basically, a new sheriff was voted in and the old sheriff didn't want to give up his position. The old sheriff was eventually removed but he came back with a mob that took the courthouse over. During the surrender of the building a black man allegedly shot a white man while walking out the building, which started another massacre resulting in many black deaths, approximately 150.

On September 30, 1919, in Elaine, Arkansas there was another massacre. Black sharecroppers were being robbed by the landowners and decided to form a union and hire a lawyer to fight the landowners. They decided to have a meeting in a church, and they knew having black people congregating would attract attention, so they had armed men guarding the church. The meeting did cause attention and a commotion started resulting in the death of a white man. The black people outnumbered the white people in this area, but white people had control of the media thereby setting the narrative. When word got out, it was said that the blacks were starting a revolution. This caused armed white men to come into Elaine, Arkansas by the hundreds. Hundreds of black people died, and five white men died. Not one person was charged for the hundreds of black deaths, but many black men were killed, beaten, and tortured to give false confessions and incarcerated over the deaths of the five white men.

While I am thinking about media influence, on September 22, 1906, in Atlanta, Georgia another massacre happened. This one happened because black men allegedly raped several white women. Once the story hit the papers, mobs formed; and they randomly attacked any black man they saw and destroyed their town. This massacre lasted three days resulting in about 100 black deaths. Many would argue the real reason was because of job competition and a lot of black people in that area were very successful.

On January 1, 1923, a massacre happened because of another alleged raping of a white woman in Rosewood, Florida. In another thriving black town, a black man was accused of raping a white woman. Mobs formed to apprehend the man. The town was destroyed, and many black people were killed. At first, it was reported that 8 black men were killed and 2 white. But some eyewitnesses say the death toll was higher, maybe about 100. What made this incident different was that there were just about the same number of dead white men as there were black men. This massacre lasted a week.

These are just a few examples of the massacres in this country that are known. I'm sure there are more buried in

185

history that this country doesn't want revealed. This country is plagued with acts of violence toward black people. These acts of violence are not limited to large groups of people or towns like previously described but to individuals, even children.

In 1955, A Chicago kid went to Mississippi to visit relatives. He decided to go to the store with his cousins to get some candy. While at the store, he whistled at the storeowner's wife. He wasn't from the area and didn't know about the "rules" of the south, so he was puzzled when his cousins dragged him out the store and rushed him home. The wife of the storeowner told her husband that a black boy came into the store and accosted her, grabbing her hand and her waist. The husband, wife, his brother, along with others tracked the boy down. The wife positively identified the boy, so they kidnapped the boy from his uncle's home. The boy was taken to a barn a few miles away where he was beaten and tortured. The boy was hit in the face and the head with what is believed to have been an axe, he had his teeth knocked out, he was shot in the head, then had a 200 pound fan tied to his neck with barbed wire and tossed in a river. Many eyewitnesses, including the boy's uncle, positively identified Roy Bryant, J.W Milam, and Carol Bryant as members of the party that kidnapped the boy. Because of the eyewitnesses, Roy Bryant and Milam went to trial. Even though there were multiple eyewitnesses, Bryant and Milam were found not guilty by an all-white, all-male jury after just an hour of deliberating. Because of what is called "Double Jeopardy", the two later on confessed to the kidnapping and murder of the boy in order to make a profit from a magazine selling the story. The 14-year-old boy was named Emmett Till.

The massacres and riots I just mentioned happened in the late 1800 and early 1900s. These are the events that have been documented. There are many more that have been purposely buried in history. The tragedy that happened to Emmett Till occurred in 1955. Though there were many incidents like this back then, this was the main one that caused the "Civil Rights Movement". This movement attempted to end racism, segregation, disenfranchisement, and discrimination. Some of the main figures in this movement were Martin Luther King, Malcolm X, Rosa Parks, Muhammad Ali, Medgar Evers and many more. The movement was a success, for the most part, everyone in the world was now aware of what was going on in this country and there was some equality. But prejudice, racism and inequality still exist today, and the violence remains.

In 1998 in Texas, three white men dragged James Byrd Jr. to his death behind a pickup truck. Byrd knew one of the men who offered him a ride home, so Byrd accepted. Instead of taking the man home, they drove off the road, beat James, urinated and defecated on him, spray painted his face, then chained him to the back of the pickup truck by his ankles and dragged him for three miles. The men left his body in front of a black church, then attended a barbeque. Instead of meeting the same fate as Emmett Till's perpetrators who were found not guilty, the civil rights movement caused all the three men to be found guilty. One is serving a life sentence in prison and the other two were executed, one in 2011 and the other 2019.

In February of 2012 in Florida, a 17-year-old teen named Trayvon B. Martin was walking back to his stepmother's house from the store when a man from the neighborhood watch saw him and called the police on him saying Trayvon looked "Suspicious". The neighborhood watchman got out of his car and followed Trayvon, after the police dispatcher told him to stay in his car. Trayvon began to run, and the watchman chased him. Trayvon even hid in some bushes trying to get away from the stranger, but the watchman still pursued him. Trayvon ran, he hid, he did everything he could do to get away from the watchman, with nothing else he could do, Trayvon stood his ground and defended himself. In the middle of the altercation, the watchman pulled out a gun and shot Trayvon, killing him. There was a trial, and the watchman was found not guilty. This grown man saw a black kid he didn't know, and felt he had the authority to approach this kid and question him. He chased the kid down, got into an altercation he was obviously losing, and shot the kid. Then, with the history of this country, he got away with it. This scumbag also went on to profit from his murder. He sold the weapon used to kill Trayvon for a sum between 130,000-250,000 dollars. He's been on book tours and helped make a movie called "The Trayvon Hoax". He even attempted to sue the Martin Family for 100 million dollars in damages but was unsuccessful. Since then, the watchman has been arrested numerous times with no convictions, he's been beaten up and shot at.

In 1944, a 14-year-old child by the name of George J. Stinney was convicted for the murder of two girls. He was held in jail for over 80 days, he was denied counsel until the day of the trial and wasn't allowed to see his parents until after the trial and conviction. George claimed the officers starved him and bribed him with food to confess. The boy went to trial which only lasted two and a half hours. His lawyer did nothing for him! He didn't have any witnesses take the stand in George's defense, even though a relative said she was with George at the time of the murder. He didn't cross-examine anyone, even though one of the investigators said it appeared the bodies had been moved. He didn't even appeal the conviction that came back from a deliberation that took ten minutes. His own lawyer was against him! George was in a courtroom where the only black person that was allowed in was the one on trial. George was executed by electric chair on June 16, 1944. He was so small he couldn't fit in the chair properly, they used a Bible for him to sit on to act as a booster seat. Through all of that, there were rumors of a prominent white family's involvement with the case, but there was no evidence. In 2014, seventy years later George Stinney was exonerated of this crime due to lack of evidence and an unfair trial.

In 1960, a 6-year-old girl name Ruby Bridges desegregated a school in New Orleans, Louisiana. She and her mother were escorted to the school by 4 U.S marshals. When Ruby got past the mob of people throwing things at her and yelling racial slurs and death threats, she was met by threats of workers poisoning her food and a woman frightening her, showing her a black baby doll in a coffin. She then was faced with people taking their children out of the class she was in, and all her teachers refusing to teach her except one, Barbara Henry. These heinous people did all this to a 6-year-old child. Ruby persevered through all of that at such a young age. She is another example of how strong and courageous women are. This 6-year-old girl carried black people on her shoulders. She got us a step further into integration. Ruby Bridges is still alive today and is an activist and she still lives in New Orleans.

The injustices of the past weren't always so brutal and blatant. As I mentioned before our people weren't allowed to leave property to their family when they passed away, that land was taken from them when the one who purchased it passed away. If their land couldn't be taken from them that way, other ways were devised. From the mid-18th century to the early 19th century, black farmers had their land taken from them because of old laws and loopholes. Between 1910-1997, our people have lost almost all of their farmland, most of it stolen. In the case Pigford Vs Glickman, the USDA wouldn't give black farmers the same loans and assistance it gave white farmers. As a result of this many black farmers lost their land. Black farmers took the USDA to court and, in the trial, representatives from the USDA admitted to denying black farmers loans and they were sued for 2 billion dollars. That's all good but the damage had already been done, land taken forever. Why wasn't the land simply given back? It has been estimated because of certain laws, fraud, and theft our people have had nearly 12 million acres of land stolen. Unfortunately, this theft is a practice that continues today.

There is a big disparity of wealth between black and white families in this country. It has been estimated that white families in America make twelve times more than the average black family. The average white family makes

190

about $175,000 while the average black family makes about $20,000. There are many reasons for this, some of which I have already mentioned. I think exploitation of slavery was one of the biggest reasons. Our people worked so hard and got nothing for it but broken promises. Families were supposed to get land and a mule. The land was given, then taken away. Even more of a slap in the face was the fact that slave owners were compensated for the end of slavery. So basically, no money was given to the people who did all the work. The money went to the people who were already making all the money. Sorry to tell you, William, but this too is a practice that continues today.

There are policies in place in certain institutions to keep our people deprived and, at the same time, increase that wealth gap. The average black family cannot walk into a bank and get loans for houses in certain neighborhoods. This practice is called "redlining". Basically the bank will not give out a loan for houses based only on the houses' locations. Even if the person is financially qualified, they still cannot get the loan. So now that family is stuck where they are, or they have to work harder and save more in order to get what that white family can get just because it's a different neighborhood. This deprives that black family of better living, better schools, better job opportunities, not to mention the frustrations and stress it causes from not getting what the bank promised if they did everything right.

Exclusion is another factor adding to this wealth gap. While many institutions play the diversity game (meaning they hire people outside their race), they still exclude our people from certain positions. We can get through the door starting at those low positions out of college, we can put the time in, work hard, do everything right and still get passed up for those promotions time and time again, even if qualified. I have even heard of people getting the excuse that they were overqualified for certain positions. So basically that means they were qualified for that job in the past. Depending on the job you get, son, sometimes you are going to work twice as hard as others and get half of what they get.

These are just some of the factors contributing to the wealth gap in the country. There are many more, these are just the more common or popular reasons in my opinion.

Why am I telling you all this, and going into greater detail with some things, you might be wondering? To say it blatantly this is being black in America. It is the year 2020 and things have not changed since some of the tragic times I mentioned! Even today two white men can kill someone like Ahmaud Arbery and be home that night to have dinner with their families. They were charged months after the incident. Even today, a white man can kill Trayvon Martin and get away with it. Even today, a cop can kill Tamir Rice and not only avoid going to jail but almost be rehired. Even today, cops can kill Breonna Taylor and not be charged for her death but instead be charged for endangering her neighbors. Even today, a cop can kill Philando Castile on tape and be acquitted of all charges. Even today, you can save up every dime you have and buy the property of your dreams only to have it taken away from you. Even today, a bank can deny you a loan because you want a house in a "white" neighborhood. Even today you can graduate college at the top of your class and be passed up by a failing student, all this because you are black.

William,

YOU ARE TRAYVON MARTIN

YOU ARE GEORGE STINNEY

YOU ARE EMMETT TILL

YOU ARE TAMIR RICE

YOU ARE PHILANDO CASTILE

YOU ARE GEORGE FLOYD

YOU ARE MICHAEL BROWN

YOU ARE FREDDIE GRAY

YOU ARE AHMAUD ARBERY

YOU ARE ERIC GARNER

YOU ARE OSCAR GRANT

YOU ARE WALTER SCOTT

YOU ARE BREONNA TAYLOR

YOU ARE ATATIANA JEFFERSON

YOU ARE STEPHON CLARK

YOU ARE BOTHAM JEAN

YOU ARE ALTON STERLING

YOU ARE AKAI GURLEY

YOU ARE AMADOU DIALLO

YOU ARE EZELL FORD

YOU ARE SAMUEL DUBOSE

YOU ARE JAMAR CLARK

YOU ARE JAMES BYRD

You are the thousands of black people that have had their lives taken away.

The majority of this country is white. Which makes America a "white nation". Yes, America is a "melting pot" but it is predominantly white. The majority in this country has a hard time accepting these facts and would instead act as if it never happened by either ignoring it, changing the narrative, or rewriting it. Racism (in the most blatant form), systemic racism and prejudice is still very much alive in this country and I strongly doubt it will go away anytime soon.

But son, don't think you will only experience racism or hate from white people. You may experience it from every ethnic group in this world. You will even experience hate from your own ethnic group or your "so called" friends. On July 6, 2012, a 16-year-old girl by the name of Skylar Neese was brutally murdered by her two best friends. They were all from West Virginia and one day drove to an area in Pennsylvania to hang out. They all used to drive to this area to hang out and smoke weed, so it wasn't unusual for them to be there. Skylar had a disagreement with the other two and thought they were going to sort everything out. Instead of talking things out, the two stabbed her over 50 times or as one of the girls said, "we stabbed her until she stopped making that gurgling noise." The two friends confessed that they had been planning out the murder for months.

Even family members can cause you harm. Unfortunately, for a good majority of disturbed people their abuse started at home. Mental abuse, physical abuse, sexual abuse, and so on often starts in their homes at a young age. If that's not bad enough, to the abused person this becomes normal life and some of them start to abuse others. This could explain why some people do some of the evil things they do. But it's never known until it is revealed.

There will always be a reason for someone to hate you or dislike you, whether it is a stranger, a friend, or a family member. Your skin may be too light or too dark. You may be too tall or too short. You may be too pretty or ugly. Trust me, people will find a reason or make up a reason to hate you.

Son, this is a hard fact of life. In order to be prepared for life you have to know the truth:

As a black man in America, you look suspicious.

As a black man in America, you look like you're up to no good.

As a black man in America, you can be killed in the street and that killer can be home that night having dinner with their family like it's a regular evening.

As a black man in America, you are guilty before being found innocent.

As a black man in America, you're a threat even with handcuffs on.

As a black man in America, you can go to jail for nothing.

As a black man in America, you don't belong in this thriving neighborhood. Who are you?

As a black man in America, you are not supposed to be in this luxury apartment building. Who are you here to see?

As a black man in America, you are not supposed to have this nice car. Whose car is this? Did you steal it?

As a black man in America, wow you have a nice position in this company. Affirmative Action must be nice.

As a black man in America…get up against the wall, "Okay fellas I know one of y'all got drugs on you?"

As a black man in America, how many baby mamas you got?

As a black man in America, why are you in this store? I don't think you can afford anything here.

As a black man in America, let me follow you so you don't shoplift.

196

As a black man in America, you can be cut in line as if you were never there.

As a black man in America, you can fight for this country in war and when you come back home, you can be hung.

As a black man in America, you can help this country become a superpower and get nothing for it.

As a black man in America, everyone can benefit except your people and it should be accepted.

As a black man in America, "hey let me tell you this hilarious joke. Why don't sharks eat black people? Because they think you are whale shit!"

As a black man in America... you made it! You are a billionaire with a good reputation and what...? You take care of your children. You are a great person a role model. "BUT you still a nigger."

As a black man in America you hear, "nigger, nigger, nigger; I have a freedom of speech."

As a black man in America, you are the one that is supposed to turn the other cheek.

As a black man in America, "We gave you your president. We are even now."

As a black man in America, get used to that look of hate in their eyes even though you never met them before.

As a black man in America, the justice system wasn't written for people like you.

As a black man in America, they won't let you forget you were once 3/5 of what they are.

As a black man in America, your aggression is hostile but the white man's aggression is instrumental.

As a black man in America, YOU DON'T BELONG UP HERE.

This is what it is like being black in America. These are the things many black people go through, some on a daily basis. This not only comes from white people but people from other races, including our own. There are some awful black people in this world, just like there are awful people in all the other races! Don't let the small number of idiots in these groups make you think this is how that whole race is. By doing that you are saying it is okay for the worst people in our race to represent the whole race. Judge each person by who they are. There are some amazing and great white people in the world just like there are amazing people in all the other races. Judge a person by who they are as an individual. Trust me, it's not the good times that will reveal their character, it's the bad times. Those times of despair, or those times a person from another race has wronged them. That is the moment you will see the real them. What comes out of their mouths in that moment of anger is how they really feel.

They say to live the American dream you have to work hard. I wish I could tell you that's true. The fact of the matter is you can work hard all your life, do everything right, and still come up short. While people who have done nothing get everything handed to them, including that

198

American dream. In America, you can do the hard work and it can pay off, just to have someone come along and take it all away from you. Sharing this with you is not to discourage you, but again to tell you the truth. By no means am I suggesting you give up or do nothing. Working hard may not give you everything you want or desire, but it will provide some important things like food and shelter. But I promise you this, son, if you constantly give up and never do anything, you will never get anything. Or as it says in the Bible, 2 Thessalonians 3:10 "If a man will not work he shall not eat." There are no promises in this country or world, and life is unfair. But every time you get knocked down, you get back up. You either are now, or will soon be, a man; take pride in that! Don't ever get knocked down and stay down because of unfair treatment, racism, sexism or anything else! Stand up!

The world is rough, there have been countless times in history where you can see man's inhumanity to man. Our people have suffered greatly in this country from this inhumanity. We can justifiably blame other racists for some of the problems we have such as poverty and lack of education. But our race has to take some accountability for how some things are today. What I mean is we have to stop blaming white people for every problem in our race, especially today in the new millennium.

Though some self-improvement issues are getting better, we have a long way to go. The highest in all crimes in this country is black on black crime. Some would argue it's the white man putting the gun in that black kid's hand. I don't know how true that is, but it's not the white man forcing the kid to pull the trigger.

Our race still has a hard time supporting one another. We can walk into a black owned establishment and be so critical of everything, especially food prices and look for a "hook-up". But we never go into McDonalds or a Chinese restaurant or pizzeria looking for a "hook-up". People don't realize prices are higher in black owned business because that establishment doesn't have the support of a chain, or their loan has higher interest.

When a black person is doing well, here comes the jealousy or the discontinued support. "This dude thinks he's better than us! I'm not gonna help him get richer." But will go to the mall and buy the newest pair of Nikes, making that billionaire richer.

Our people don't value family like other races, as far as parenting goes. Again, it's improving slightly but our men still don't want to take care of their children. Other races do have some issues with this, but nothing like our race. I still don't understand why men don't want to take care of their children, leaving our women to do it all. If more of our men supported their children, I think many of the issues plaguing our race would get better.

Even in some black homes that have both parents, I sometimes notice parents tell their children at a certain age they have to leave the house and find their own way, with nothing. No other race puts their children on the street with nothing. Just ours! In other races, they help their children or family financially even when they leave the house. This is part of the reason why you see Asian Indians come to this country with nothing and then 3 years later they own a store and a house. It is the support of their family and support of our government (ummm yeaaa it's easier for an immigrant to get support from our government than us).

Well, there it is William, this could be your America. You could experience racism and a lack of support or hate from your own. Actually, at some point in your life, you will experience some form of discrimination, racism (blatant or systemic), sexism, or hate from your own people or some kind of unfair treatment; so prepare yourself. You must adapt and get through it because you have to go out in the world to live. Once you get through the obstacles and reach your goal, that's when you have to be extra vigilant because that's when people strategically begin to come at you.

 Like the gazelle in the wild that must get to the water source to live, it must get past the lions stalking it. Once the gazelle gets to the water before it drinks it has to look around because when it's drinking it is vulnerable. Is the objective complete, is the gazelle safe? NO! Yes, it made it to the water and now it is drinking. But it still has to stay alert and, when done drinking, go back through the path of lions. What about the crocodile that has been signaled because the gazelle disturbed the water? It now has another predator to deal with.

William, you are that gazelle. One day you will be headed for that goal through a path full of predators. The closer you get to that goal, the more predators stalk you. You have to find ways to identify and avoid them and stay on the path. Once you achieve that goal, there will be predators in your water. Which is to say, there will be people trying to take all that you have or trying to destroy you. Stay alert son, please understand as a free black man in this country, you are an endangered species.

Life for our people has been hard since the first day introduced to this country, and it continues today despite what people try to persuade you to believe. Understand and believe that there are two different Americas. While issues today aren't as bad as they were in the past, they still exist; and you have to navigate through them. This country is not alone in the bad treatment of our people, in fact this is a global problem. Racism and genocide in Africa are far worse than in the United States, for example. What I'm trying to say is, no matter where you go in this world, you will always be looked down on, as black man. You are stuck in this skin! What do you do? You Embrace it! You hold your head up and stick your chest out! You eventually understand people try to keep you down because you are better than them and they know it! They fear that, if you get a full head of steam, you will take over. They are right!

The two things I find most frustrating today is the racial division in this country and how hard people try to take God out of everything. I have never seen the country more divided than it is today. There is such racial tension that I wouldn't be surprised if a race war happened at any second. Today, your political view determines what type of racist you are. If you are a conservative, you are a white racist. If you are progressive, you are a black racist. We are so busy fighting one another that no one is benefitting. History has proven to us that working together we achieve so many things. Alfred Blalock, a white surgeon and Vivien Thomas, his black assistant, together helped end blue baby syndrome. Creola K. Johnson, a black mathematician, helped NASA get the United States into space. If the playing field was made even, and black people reaped the same benefits as white people, I feel this country would have the best economy in the world. No social class in the country benefits from homelessness. If more people had money, more money would be spent making the economy better for everyone. Instead of moving forward together, making new discoveries, and fixing problems; we are hating one another because of our differences. America is losing.

Another big issue I have is the great lengths people have gone to remove the name God out of things. Some people are even trying to get the "In God We Trust" off the U.S. currency. In my opinion, things started going bad in this country when we started doing things like this. No more prayer in public schools, no more saying, "Merry Christmas." Why? I haven't seen one positive thing happen since this practice has started. I am a strong believer in God, and I feel this country needs God more than ever now. Perhaps, if we included God more in this country, things would start to improve.

Life Rules

As I mentioned in the previous section, no matter where you go or what you do, you will always be black. People from other races are always going to think you're angry. When they see you walking up the street toward them, most are going to walk across the street to the other side. When you get in a Jacuzzi, all the white people are going to get out. I guess they think you're going to turn the water into tea or something.

As you get older you will be a witness to some of the things I wrote about, though I pray you won't. I pray that, by the time you become a man, you won't experience any of this negativity. It seems this country can't move on from this destruction. Life doesn't always have to be hard and sometimes it's not, life can be very good. No matter which way it goes, you have to prepare yourself. Here are some of ways I have prepared myself for life with the help of my friends and family. These are my morals and values or rules I live by. No order of importance, just writing how I'm thinking about it.

-Never Quit.

-Love yourself.

-Have fun in life.

-Always leave a nice tip.

-Be independent.

-Treat others like you want to be treated.

-Life is unfair.

-Conduct around cops.

-Don't only clean your house when guests are coming over.

-Take pride in what you have and in your appearance.

-Speak when people speak to you.

-Control your actions.

-Don't take anger out on everyone.

-When invited to someone's house never go empty-handed.

-How to shake a man's hand.

-Find a trade.

-Find a job you love.

-Make goals then a plan.

-Have 3 plans for important things in life.

-Cherish good friends.

-Always keep in touch with family and friends.

-Standup for yourself.

-Be careful how you approach people and things.

-Vote.

-Learn people.

-Try to always be a good person.

-Never hate for no reason.

-Buy a gun.

-Don't glorify stupidity.

-Seek the truth.

-Practice makes perfect.

-Become the best father you can.

-Home is more important than work.

-Always make your home a place of peace.

-Go on vacation.

-Don't let anyone change you.

-Be careful of the company you keep.

-If you do the crime, you have to do the time.

-Don't let anyone define you.

Never Quit! Never Quit! This is more than a saying. When there is something in life that you want, or a destination that you absolutely must get to, you gotta go get it! Don't ever let the obstacles get in the way of something you want. If there's something in life you really want, nothing is going to stand in your way, if you really want it. I wanted to be a firefighter all my life. I was going to be a firefighter! I was out in the freezing weather in feet of snow practicing for the physical. No obstacle was going to stand in my way. That's how you have to be son. You have to get it in your mind that you have to go out in the world and get what you want. It's not going to be easy, some things are going to be extremely difficult to obtain. But you have to go get it! Nothing easy in life is worth cherishing.

No matter what, always take time for yourself. Treat yourself to a steak dinner or buy yourself that coat you want. There aren't too many people in the world to love you, so love yourself! Treat yourself well and spoil yourself often. Go on multiple vacations or a weekend getaway, go to a spa if that's your thing. Life, at times, becomes complicated; don't let it get so bad that you forget to take care of yourself. People will come into your life claiming they love you. Some of them will, some won't. There is one person who will always love you and that is you. Love yourself!

As I just mentioned, life has a way of becoming tough sometimes. There will always be more important things to do than others, despite this, make time to have fun in life. Smile often, do something fun often, do things you enjoy often. If you wake up upset in the morning or don't laugh at least once a day, you are doing something wrong.

When you go out to a restaurant, if the service is good and you see your waiter working hard, leave them a nice tip and show them some respect. Just because they are serving you doesn't mean they are beneath you. They are handling your food, which is another reason to treat them well.

Son, please don't be one of these men out here expecting his woman to take care of him. Your woman is supposed to be your girlfriend or wife, not your mother. As a man, you are supposed to take care of your woman, in my opinion. There's nothing worse than seeing a grown capable man being taken care of by a woman. This woman goes out and works, takes care of the children, then comes home to cook and clean, while this lazy man sits around the house doing nothing productive all day. Don't be that poor excuse for a man. Make your own money so you don't have to ever worry about this woman kicking you out. You are more attractive to a woman when you have your own money.

Treat others like you want to be treated. This saying is self-explanatory. Everyone wants to be respected, but if you want to be respected, you must show respect. If you want people to be understanding toward you, you must be understanding toward them. Don't expect to go through life treating people any way you want, without someone coming along treating you any way they want. Don't be a hypocrite.

I hope you picked up on this earlier in the book, but life is unfair. You can do something right 1000 times but mess up just once and lose everything. You can be a nice guy over and over again, and constantly get the short end of the stick. In this world, people play by their own rules. Go into every situation or relationship knowing this. Please understand you can accept a person in your life and treat them the best you can just for that person to stab you in the back one day for no reason. Go into every relationship with good intentions and try to be a good person, at the same time, be cautious. A person's true intents will one day be revealed. The only bad thing is it may take years to see.

This is very important; when a cop encounters you, you show that officer respect. You do not give them attitude, you do not tell them what the law says, and you do not offend the officer. If driving, you pull your car over, you turn on the lights, roll down the windows and place your hands where the officer can see them at all times. You do not move your hands until the officer tells you to. Comply with the officer, so they don't kill you, son. However, if a cop ever asks if they can search you or any of your possessions the answer is always no! Don't help them arrest you. Whatever you do, make sure you remain calm and do not make any sudden movements. If you have a grievance with the officer, you ask for his commander or get his name and take it to the police station to file a report. You make sure that report is filed so it is on their record. If you should get arrested, again remain calm. Do not say anything to a police officer without an attorney present. Remember you have a right to remain silent, use that right. The cops interrogating you will use what you say against you. They will try any fair or unfair tactic to pin a crime on you. Do not trust a cop no matter what they say, a cop interrogating you is not a friend. Let the lawyer speak for you.

Don't only clean your house when guests are coming over. Why should you treat a person that doesn't live in the house better than you treat the people who do live in the house? Clean your house for you and the people that live with you. Take pride in your house. Don't think of it as a chore. Be grateful you have home to clean.

Take pride in your appearance. At some point in life, you might not have the money to spend on fancy clothes. That doesn't mean you have to look nor dress poorly, or not shave or comb your hair. Iron the clothes you have, trim your beard if you have one, and comb or brush your hair. You might not have the money to go to a laundromat, so wash your clothes in your bathtub. You do what you have to, and you do it with your head up. Don't let circumstances define who you are. If you have to be at a place early in the morning like school, for instance, get your clothing out the night before so you can make sure it looks nice, or in case you need to iron. Don't plan certain engagements if you don't have the appropriate attire to attend or the means to get it. Don't plan a job interview, if you don't have a suit or a decent pair of pants or a shirt and tie. Take pride in your appearance. If you don't like the beer gut you have, stop drinking and do some sit-ups. And please for God's sake, do not wear your pants hanging off your ass like these dudes out in the street with their drawers showing. I have never seen one of them accomplish anything with their pants hanging off their asses like that. They look like fools! Do your best to look nice, be neat, and dress appropriately for the occasion.

Speak when people speak to you. It is rude and ungentlemanly for a person to go out of their way to greet you and for you to walk past them or not acknowledge them. Even if you are having the worst day ever, you still need to speak. This person has no idea what's going on in your life, so don't blame them for the rough time you are having. There are times when speaking to that person might help you. They may speak words of wisdom to you that may help you get through whatever it is you're going through. So, acknowledge them, and don't let anything in your life get you out of character.

Another important point is to always control your actions. You may not be able to control your emotions; something a person does or says to you may hurt you and you can't control how you feel about that. But you can control your actions regarding what happens next. You may be confronted with a situation where you can throw hands or walk away. A greater majority of the time, the best thing to do is walk away. Making an emotional decision when in a highly tense situation can put you in serious trouble. Just that split second, a loss of control is all it takes to put you in jail or have someone kill you. Even during times of temptation (something I will always struggle with), you have to control your actions. It's better to walk away from the donuts, than to eat the whole dozen for example. You might be tempted to sell drugs because you're short on money or rob someone because you're hungry. Don't do it! Control your actions, walk away, and come up with a better solution.

While controlling your actions make sure you don't take your anger out on everyone. While it is okay to feel anger or be angry, direct that anger or leave that anger where it originated. If you are angry about something that happened at school, don't come home and take that anger out on your mom, grandmother, or family pet. Go for a walk, play a sport or vent to a friend. Find out why it angers you or come up with a solution to fix the problem. Do not take your anger out on someone or something that had nothing to do with that situation and certainly never take your anger out violently, for reasons stated before.

When you are invited to someone's house for some type of gathering, never go empty-handed. Stop by a store and get a bottle of wine, grab a dessert like a baked good or cook one of your fan favorites, and bring it. It is considerate and shows class if you contribute to the party.

When greeted by another man, if you are seated, stand up; look him in his eyes; and give him a firm right-handed shake. That is the way men say hello. Don't hand him a "dead fish" or a limp handshake while looking down at his feet, which shows weakness or a lack of confidence. Stand up, look him in his eyes, and squeeze his hand like you trying to stop the blood from flowing and do it with a slight smile. Now for a lady same format; however, do not squeeze her hand but grab it firmly and give her a bigger smile. If she is single and cute, give her hand a slight twist and kiss the back of her hand. For children, give them a high five.

In our community, going to college is a big deal. It's viewed as a privilege and the way to go if you want to have a successful life. What they didn't know or failed to tell you was that while part of that is sometimes true, it leaves you in debt for the first 15 years of your new independent life. To make matters worse you may not find a job coming out of college. I recommend that before going to college you pick up a trade. I have seen many college grads not be able to find work for years, but I rarely see a person that studied a trade out of work. I even see people who studied a trade making more money than the college grad. I have seen people holding two degrees working at the mall. But I have never seen a plumber working at the mall. I have seen people in trades opening their own business in 5 years, but I've never seen a college grad start their own business at all. I see college grads working for temp companies and on unemployment lines, but I've never seen an electrician out of work. I'm not saying don't go to college, what I am saying is consider a trade before going. People need plumbers, electricians, or HVAC techs before they need marketers or advertisers. Always have something to fall back on or a plan "B" just in case one thing doesn't work out like you planned.

When you become a man, son, find a job you love. Life is much better when you are doing something you love. When you have that dream job, it sometimes does not feel like it's work at all. Be serious about it, turn it into your craft. Learn your craft and take it seriously. If you take care of your work, your work will take care of you. But take into consideration that there will be something about that job you don't particularly like. That's why they call it work and not fun. I pray you find the job of your dreams, but always have a secondary or even third source of income. Though you love this job, you could lose it or lose interest. There is nothing wrong with leaving a job you love for a better opportunity. But be careful doing that, it's not always about money. The satisfaction or good life comes from being happy doing what you're doing. It is vitally important to be happy son.

Make a goal, then make a plan to achieve that goal. Many people make the mistake of coming up with a plan and not having a goal in mind. For instance, you approach a kid in high school and ask them what their future plans are after high school. They say, "After high school, I am going to college." You say, "Oh that's good! What are you going to study?" and they reply, "I don't know." That right there is making a plan but not having a goal in mind. This comes from that mindset I talked about earlier, that going to college is how you become successful. Some people think college is the destination. I feel that's the wrong way to think about it. If there's no goal, why make a plan? You have to set a goal, then go get it. That goal can change, but you still need a direction to go in. Set the goal, then make the plan. You lay it all out, see everything involved, and make the commitment to go get it. Some things are going to be difficult to overcome in this plan. But if it were easy, everyone would do it.

I hinted at this a few times before, but always have back-up plans for things in life. Things are not always going to work out the way you want them to. You might not go to that college you've always dreamed of or you might not land that dream job. For this reason, you have to think of other ways to achieve your goals. If that dream college doesn't work you have to pick another. If that secondary college doesn't work you may have to pick a trade. The goal doesn't always have to be that dream job, but the job that will provide you with the life you want to live.

Another important thing, in life, is to cherish good friends. I have been blessed to have some of the friends I have. They have always been there for me in good and especially bad times. In those moments of life, when you feel lonely or not yourself, one of the best things to do is reach out to a friend. If they are always there for you, you have to always be there for them. Getting together and talking, or doing a favorite activity with your boys, is sometimes all you need to get back on track or clear your mind. These are some of the strongest and longest bonds you will ever make in your life. Love it, respect it, nurture it, and cherish these relationships.

Always keep in touch with friends and family. This is also an important thing in life, and a way you can nurture relationships. Simply picking up the phone seeing how a person is doing can be just what that person needs to get them through a challenging time. Just taking a few minutes to talk to someone lets him or her know you are concerned. Don't just call a person when you want or need something. Call them to check on them. Tell them you were just thinking of them and called to see how they were doing. Don't just call in bad times or holidays, call to say, "Hello how are you?" It is as simple as that.

In life, there will often be times when you have to stand up for yourself. There will always be someone trying to take advantage of you or take what you have. Unfortunately, it comes from people close to you, not always a person you don't know. It could be a friend, a girlfriend, even family trying to take something from you or persuade and manipulate you to do something for them that may hurt you. If you know it's wrong or it's something you don't agree with, stand up for yourself and don't do it. Don't let them take anything from you. They may try to take your money or one of your possessions. They may try to talk you into doing something that could get you in trouble. Don't allow them to do this without resistance. Do not allow yourself to be easily manipulated. Sometimes you have to physically fight them off if they are trying to take something from you. Other times, you simply have to walk away if they are trying to make you do something wrong like steal money or hurt someone. Don't give into peer pressure. If you know it's wrong don't do it and stay away from that person.

Be careful how you approach people and situations. Be mindful of your conduct with that person in those situations. As a man (especially a black man), at trying times, you are seen as a threat or the aggressor if an incident happens. Even if you are the victim trying to defend yourself, you are looked at as the person who initiated the altercation. Just raising your voice could make someone call the police. How tall or how muscular you are and how you approach them may lead a person to believe you mean to do them harm. When all you wanted to do was talk in order to gain some clarity or understanding. When a problem arises, most of the time, it's because of a miscommunication or misunderstanding. The way you deal with these problems is with a cool head. Try not to get frustrated and overreact. If you know the situation is getting tense it's best to walk away and let all parties cool down. However, some situations you can't avoid, you may have to fight in order to defend yourself. If that's what you have to do, you fight until you can get away or they stop moving. Be especially careful and coolheaded if any of these altercations involve women. No matter what happens, even if she initiated, everyone is going to look at you as the bad guy. Try with everything in you not to hit this woman. You should never hit a woman. It is best to handle problems with women over the phone in my opinion.

If you are of age when you read this, please make sure you VOTE. Vote in every single election you can. Anytime there's a major election in your city, it does affect you in some way. Research the candidates and vote for the person you think is best qualified for the job. Our people have gone through too much in order for our voice to be heard, because of their efforts it is our right to vote. Voting is our chance to put someone in office that will do things in our best interest. Not voting at all is one of the worst things you can do, especially in local elections. It is the local election that will affect your life everyday, not the presidential ones. So make sure you always vote.

Everyone has a reason (outside of family) for being in your life. You have to figure out what each reason is by learning this person. Some people are only in your life for a season. Those are the people in your life for a short time, not everyone is meant to stay forever. You have to figure out which are here to stay, and which are going to go. After learning about people and seeing who they really are, you may make the decision to leave them. But understand, everyone (including you) has a selfish reason for companionship. We want someone around, we want someone to talk to, we want someone to hang out with. Just because it's a selfish reason doesn't mean it's all bad. It's about "give and take". You want them there for you, you have to be there for them. You are going to unknowingly invite people in your life who just want to use you and do nothing for you. You have to see this person for what they really are and excuse them from your life.

Try to always be a good person. No matter what this world throws at you, try to remain a good person. In life, you are going to have so many challenges. There are going to be things that happen out of your control. No matter what, don't lose your integrity. This is easier said than done, though. It's easy to become angry or bitter in life. It is sometimes harder to be good. You have to try your hardest to be good. No one said life was easy.

Never hate a person for absolutely no reason. Half the problem with a lot of people in the world is that they hate people simply based on their color or religion. How can you hate a person you know nothing about? This person has never said a word to you or done anything to you, so how can you hate them? Give a person a chance and you may learn some great things about them and some great things about yourself. At least let them give you a reason to hate them.

Another thing to do when you come of age is to buy a gun. It is our 2nd amendment right, after all. Your mother probably wouldn't like for me to give you this advice because she hates guns. I didn't particularly like guns earlier in life, but as I have gotten older I think you should own a gun, several in fact. A gun is the best weapon you can have in your home for protection. A child can use the gun just as good as a 90-year-old to protect themselves. If a person breaks into your house odds are they have a gun. You cannot defend yourself against a gun by calling the police, hiding, or showing the invader a knife. History has shown us that many battles have been won or lost because of weaponry. Why not have the best weapons in your home for your protection? Get a gun, son.

Do not glorify stupidity. You can really look like an idiot praising things you know are wrong. Wearing your pants hanging off your ass is stupid. Drinking and driving is stupid. Glorifying drug dealers is stupid. Glorifying prison is stupid. Glorifying stupid people is stupid. Glorifying criminals is stupid.

Seek the truth. Don't believe everything people tell you. There are going to be so many people in the world who are going to lie to you and try to keep you from the truth. This is going to happen on a big and small scale. This happens for many reasons, but the basic reasons are that people are ashamed of something, they don't want you to know what really happened, and they don't want to face the consequences. This goes really deep in our country. There are people who actually live in Tulsa, OK, in the very place a massacre happened, and have no clue it ever happened. Things in the country that people are ashamed of, those people want the tragedies to be buried or forgotten. They either never speak of it, hoping time will help it fade; or they change the narrative to make it look as if they are the victims. The only way to truly know the answer, son, is to look for it yourself. The best way to do that is to track down people who were actually there. That's not always possible so the only other thing you can do is go to a reliable source. Reputable news sources, reputable college professors, elderly people, or educated people in your subject of interest are all great places to start your search. Listen to different points of view - the people that supply the most accurate history, connect the dots and explain the reasons why some things happened; or why things are what they are today are good sources. But you have to be honest when doing this. When some people research something, they only research what the want to be true. Basically they want to hear what they want to hear, so to speak. When you research for the truth, be ready to accept the real answer. Some things you discover you might not like, but you have to be real about it.

Practice makes perfect. In life, son, you will rarely be naturally talented at something. There will be things that you do naturally well, like run fast or jump high. Even those things you do well, you still need to practice so you can perfect it. But most things in life you are not going to be good at touching for the first time. When this time comes, the only way to get better at it is to practice. This isn't only limited to sports, this is true in many aspects of life. You can practice at a craft, you can practice meditating, you can practice a technique in a hobby, the list is endless. At times, to be honest, practicing can suck. You spend hours training when the actual event can take just 45 minutes. The thing is you practice to get better at something, so when that event happens you make it look easy. You practice to be good at whatever you're doing. Trust me, with practice you can do almost anything son.

Become the best father you can. If you decide to have children, try to be the best father possible. You don't have to have a lot of money or possessions to be a good dad. All you have to do is be there, talk to your kid (tell them the truth), and go to the plays and ball games. Take them to the movies on a school night or go out for ice cream. Be there with them in good and bad times. When you are with them, make everything look easy and fun. But when you are not with them, work hard for them. Make sure you have life and health insurance, make sure you always have emergency money, and make sure you have a plan for everything possible. A fire plan, an intruder plan, a plan when they find themselves alone, and the list goes on. Be mindful of what you do and how you conduct yourself. Remember you always have someone watching now and depending on you. So, when or if you have children, make sure you accept every possible thing that may happen including having issues with their mom and possibly not being with them. Children are a big sacrifice but well worth it. You have to be mentally, physically, and financially ready, if you think that's the route you want to go. As stated before, you don't need a lot of money, but you do need some. Now, if you want to spoil your children (which I recommend), you need a nice amount of money. So, it's a good idea to have a good job before starting a family. It is better to be married before having children but that is not the route I took, so I can't speak with experience about that way of doing things. I can say, I love taking my kids on vacations of our choice, I love buying them things they want, I love seeing their cheeks fat with food and buying them big coats for the winter. Being a father is not hard, you just have to want to do it.

Home is more important than work. People sometimes forget you go to work in order to provide a home. Home is not only the place where you live; it is the place that holds all you have and all you love. I understand loving work, loving what you do and making money, but people sometimes spend so much time at work that they sacrifice time at home. Time at home, doing what you love is precious. You can't get that time back and as you get older you are going to regret it, especially if you have a family. Spending time with the family is something I love and cherish. Do not be one of those people who look back on their lives and regret not spending more time with loved ones and doing things they loved.

Always make your home a place of peace. Work can be stressful, and life can be stressful as well. Do not let your home add to this stress. Your home should be your place of peace and tranquility. If you are having some issues with your spouse; sit down, discuss the disagreement, and make things right. There should be peace in your house for everyone that lives there. Everyone has a stressful day at times, so they should find peace when they get home. Things that need to be fixed can cause stress. Don't let things linger like a running toilet or a leaking faucet. Fixing the problem takes stress away. Don't use drinking or drugs to fix problems. These things don't fix problems, they add to them. Most of the time, the best way to solve a problem is to first admit a problem exists, then to talk it out. If the problem can't be addressed by a conversation or a plan then you have to accept the fact that some issues can't be fixed. If the issue can't be fixed, then an adjustment is needed to bring back the peace. There are also times when all you can do is pray about it and let God handle it, it is my experience that God will always bring you peace.

One thing that will often bring peace is a nice relaxing vacation. Don't look at vacationing as a luxury, look at it as a necessity. A nice vacation is a great way to unwind and take a break from all the stress. Vacationing, maybe 2 or 3 times a year, is a great way to reflect and live without all the distractions. A nice vacation is also a way to remain mentally healthy. You don't have to go away for weeks at a time (although that would be great), all you need is 3 or 4 days. If you have a wife and kids, it's a great way to catch up and be together.

Don't let anyone change you. If you keep letting people change you, you are going to lose your identity and forget who you are. Try to always be the good person you are. There will be times when people will try you and take you out of your character. For instance, if a person is constantly mean to you, don't become a mean person. It is better to delete that person from your life or avoid them before becoming them. Don't let negativity in your heart and soul. Don't become whatever negativity surrounds you. Be strong and be you.

Be careful of the company you keep. As I have just mentioned, if a person is negative, don't let that negativity into your peaceful space. Some people are only in this world to do bad things. That's all they know and that's all they are. If you associate yourself with these people, others will think you are just like them. So be careful of the people you have in your circle. If you roll with a bunch of criminals you, one day, will most likely become a criminal. You will become what you surround yourself with. Surrounding yourself with good people who want you to succeed is what you should do.

If you do the crime, be prepared to do the time. I want you to have a good life and I would love to guide you through your life, but even if I was able to be around you every day you could still go down the wrong path. Every action has a reaction, whether it's good or bad. As you get older, you have to constantly be mindful of both, your actions and reactions. If you allow your emotions to take over instead of being logical, be prepared to suffer the consequences. People who commit crimes are not always bad people. Some people commit crimes to survive, for example, a hungry person who steals food. Although they may be a good person in a dire situation, if they are caught stealing, they may suffer the consequences. So think about things before you put yourself in bad situations and always keep in mind that, if you commit a crime, you may do the time. I do not condone committing any crime, yet I do understand why people do. If you have to commit a crime, do it alone and don't tell anyone what you have done. Especially if you get away with it, don't go bragging. If you manage to get away with it, don't commit the same crime again. As I said, I don't condone it but as your father I still feel a need to protect you.

Don't let anyone define you. As you grow up, you are going to hear a lot of people give their opinion of you. Some things they say are going to be good, but most are going to be bad. Hearing someone say something good about you is nice, but it's the bad things they say that you focus and dwell on. You will question yourself and why they feel the way they do about you. You might, one day, have a teacher tell you that you won't amount to anything. They can have their opinion. They can feel however they want. That doesn't mean you have to listen to them or take to heart anything they say. Know who you are. Be the person you are going to be. Do not let anyone tell you who you are, or what you will become. Some people are going to hate you, son. These same people see the greatness in you, and they are trying to stop you from achieving it. So they put things in your head to deter you. Don't let them do this you son, go get what's yours! Don't let anyone tell you who you are.

William, this is just a tip of the iceberg of things I want to say to you. I could never sum up years of conversations into one book. At times in the past, even today, I can sit down and talk to my parents (especially my mother) about anything. Some conversations held were difficult, but most were pleasant. I plan on doing the same with my children if you all ever approach me with a concern. I want to be there for all of you. I might not be able to get to you now, but I hope these words find you. I don't know what age that might be, but I pray it is an age where you understand that I love you, I want you around, and you are my son. I pray I see you when you are still a young child, so I can watch you grow and be there with you as you develop. But I am uncertain of when or if that will happen. I have made mistakes in dealing with all of this. Perhaps there is more I could be doing for you. But I honestly don't know what other routes I can take. I have never been in a situation before where I couldn't see one of my children. It is a painful place to be. I think of you multiple times a day and worry about you. I still contact your mother weekly attempting to see you, but she never responds. I really don't know what else to do. I am not, nor will I ever give up on trying to see you though. I will be taking your mother to court again so I can see you. Round 2.

In the meantime, I will sit and wait for the day I can see you. I am making plans for the day. I figured there would be a nice party with close family and friends to welcome you. I know when I give the news that you are coming, everyone is going to want to come over and see you. We are known to have good parties, and the party for you would be one of the biggest and best. It depends on how old you are going to be when that day comes for me to fine-tune the party. Are we going to have bouncy-houses, water balloons and pizza or are we going to have prime rib, lobster, and drinks? I imagine everyone is going to want to talk to or play with you and have his or her time with you.

226

It may be overwhelming at first, but you will get a lot of attention. Then all the guests will go home but you will stay because this is your house. And you and I will talk about anything on your mind. You may come when you are 3 years old or 33 years old, it doesn't matter I will be here waiting for you and I will be ready!

TO MY BROTHERS

The last section of this book is directed to my brothers in this world (whatever race you are) who might be in a similar situation that I am in. But, William, if you find yourself in a position like this, this is for you too. I refuse to think I am the only man in this world going through this. I am being labeled a "deadbeat" because the mother of my son will not let me see him. The stigma of this country that black men don't take care of their children has fallen on me through no fault of my own. No one speaks up for the men in this world trying to do the right thing and be involved in their child's life. There might not be as many of us as there should, but we are here! But when their mother tells the story of why dad isn't here, is she going to tell the truth? Is she going to say, "He tried to be here, but I pushed him away"? I doubt it, even though that's the truth.

I tried to be with the woman with whom I share my son. I tried to be there in the hospital with my son and was removed from the hospital at his mother's discretion. I've begged this woman to see my son and I am still being ignored to this current day. I've reached out to his mother and we came up with an arrangement that she did not honor. I have reached out to this woman's family in an attempted to be in my son's life only to be called a deadbeat and to be told to stop harassing them with threats of police involvement. I have taken this woman to court in an attempt to arrange visitation and establish child support, but the court did nothing for me. So what now?

There are many different ways I could have dealt with this problem, and many thoughts crossed my mind. I thought of just giving up, I figured she obviously doesn't want me around my kid for some reason. But then I said, "No way, I can't do that to my son, I can't just give up on him. What kind of man would I be?" In this book, I told him to never give up, yet I'm giving up?? No way! I'm no hypocrite.

I thought of going to her house and just demanding to see him. The only thing that would have done is made this situation worse. Even though I would have approached peacefully, his mother would have only seen a threat. What was I really going to do anyway? Tell her how I felt about her, and she was just going to give him to me? Yea right! The cops would have been waiting for me with a restraining order when I came home, even if it was a peaceful encounter. What if he would have seen me yelling at his mother or causing a commotion? I wouldn't want the first time my son and I see each other again to be like that. I'm sure his mother would have then said, "See that was your father, this is why I don't want you to see him." Confirming the lies she may tell him when he asks about me one day.

One thing I tried was taking the matter to court, but I feel it didn't work for me. I felt it was a big waste of time and, worse, money. While I thought my lawyer was good, I think I could have done better speaking for myself. No one knew my case better than me. But I was not going against a lawyer who hired a lawyer in court without some legal representation. I felt they would try to take advantage of me, which they tried to do previously in mediation. Though

I am reluctant to do so, I will most likely be taking the matter back to court, if this alienation continues. I will not give up on trying to see my son, even if I have to go through the courts again. This was my courtroom experience, perhaps others have had better results. This may be the only legal way to be with your child, so you have to go for it. Perhaps the first time you were unsuccessful. There's really nothing else you can do but try again. Later on in this section, I'm going to list a few things men can do in preparation of going to court.

Another thing you can do is reach out to your child. Perhaps they are old enough to listen and understand what is going on and willing to give you the opportunity to tell your side of the story. There are a few options to do this: a phone call, writing a letter, or reaching out on social media. This may be the only way you can tell your side of the story or tell your truth.

My son is currently too young to read letters or have an account on any social media platform and his mother is not going to let me talk to him on the phone. So, what I have decided to do is write a book telling him things I think a father should discuss with his son and my side of the story. Writing this book has helped me vent my frustrations of not being able to see him. It also, in a way, allows me to talk to him. Obviously, I am not getting a response but as I write I imagine his facial expressions as he thinks about what I wrote and his responses. Prayerfully, one day he will read this book before we meet, and I don't have to imagine his response but instead he and I can have a conversation about it. I hope as he reads he understands that I did not abandon him, and I would love very much to have a relationship with him. If he is still too young to read it when we meet, I will read it to him and his brother.

COURT

At times, in order to see your child you may have to go to court. I am going to give a few suggestions of what you can do to help with your courtroom war, as well as make you aware of some things. I am not going to go into great detail because I am not a lawyer. Each state is different, I don't want to steer you down the wrong path and I want you to do your own research. I would suggest trying to resolve issues of not seeing your child out of court, if you can; but if you have no other alternative you may have to go to court. This is just my experience and what I have learned. This is intended for men who are having issues seeing their children through no fault of their own. This is not for those who are being taken to court for not paying child support or other self-inflicted issues.

The first thing you want to do is make sure the child is yours. I have seen men go to court and get into the war for months, just to find out the children aren't theirs. You cannot get your money back for legal expenses and it's a waste of time. It is even more painful if the child isn't yours and you get attached. The child is not biologically yours, now you have no rights to the child at all. Before any of this happens, just get a simple cheek swab DNA test. You may have to go through the courts to get testing done, but judges usually grant this pretty easily.

Before you think of going to court, ask yourself, "Why won't she let me see my child?" If you abused this woman, this child or have a history of abuse don't even bother going to court until you get yourself some help. Once you get the help you need, you may have a better chance in court. If you are serious about seeing your kid, you will get the help you need.

As I mentioned before, laws are different from state to state and some are not very favorable for men. But in all states, men do have some rights. You have to research and ask a lawyer which rights apply to your case. In most states, men cannot be denied visitation without a good reason. The mother cannot keep your child from you just because she's upset with you. In some places, the mother cannot move out of the state and take the child without the father's consent. Doing some research and finding out your rights will help you greatly in court. It may even prevent going to court if presented beforehand.

Going to court is a very emotional thing. Be prepared to be stressed out, frustrated, and hurt. Going to court with a woman you use to make love to is bad enough, but when you add a child to the mix it hurts more. The case can also move very slowly depending on all the evidence both parties bring before the judge and one party's procrastination. My trial lasted a year because of these two issues and a few more. So, take that into consideration before filing.

You can represent yourself in court (pro se) if you have some knowledge of how things work in court, along the lines of filing applications and/or complaints, litigations, court procedures, and discovery, to name a few. Even with some knowledge, I strongly recommend getting a lawyer. Some courts even find it disrespectful if you don't. Keep in mind, some judges are not going to help you understand things discussed in the case. You may need a lawyer with you, so the adversary doesn't take advantage of you. You are already behind the 8-ball, being a man in court. Don't make it worse. Some courts may help you because you are alone but why take the chance? You might only have one shot to get it right. There are different rules and laws in each state. It would be a good idea to look up the laws of the state where you are going to court, to better prepare yourself. There are tons of self-help law literature out there, you simply have to do the research.

Research some family lawyers who are familiar with the laws in the state where you are going to court. Most lawyers or law firms allow you to get one consultation for free. Before you visit that lawyer, think of all the questions you want to ask and be honest about what is going on. Do not lie to your lawyer, and do not leave anything out, even if you are ashamed or embarrassed about it. Make sure you tell the lawyer all you are attempting to gain from court. Do you want sole custody, joint custody, or visitation? Whatever it is you are trying to gain, let the lawyer know. It's a good idea for you to try to establish child support, if that's an issue. It makes you look better to the judge.

There are times you can go to court and not go to trial. This is when both parties can come to some kind of agreement before going to trial. I advise you to do all you can to sort things out in this stage. It will save you a lot of heartache and money. However, don't be taken advantage of in this stage. If things aren't looking good to you or you aren't getting anything you want, don't sign anything! This is a negotiation stage, some things you win and some you lose but you shouldn't lose on everything. Just take it to trial.

When you have the meeting with the lawyer, be well groomed and dress nicely. A nice haircut and a nice button-down shirt and pants or a suit will do. This should be the same way you dress for court. Bring a notepad of some kind, with your questions in it and a couple of pens to take notes. Ask the lawyer every question you have and, if you don't understand something, ask the lawyer to explain. Do not leave without having a full understanding of what is going on. Make sure you mention everything you have attempted and everything that has happened. You can do this with more than one firm. Look around until you find the lawyer with whom you are most comfortable.

Research the lawyer you are thinking about picking. At times, people write reviews about lawyers. Read all of them! This can be tremendously helpful for you. You can avoid some issues in the future. For example, some lawyers aren't very good, some have so many cases that they don't give your case the attention you think it deserves, and some have a bad reputation with certain judges and courthouses. Reading reviews can help you prevent a lot of lost time and money.

The lawyer you pick should be able to tell you how the laws work in that state. In some states, for example, you have to go through mediation before court, whereas in other states you don't have to go through mediation. Mediation is a good thing, it's the court's way of trying to have both parties sort things out without lawyers in most cases. If it works out, that's a great thing, and you fix things without having a trial.

If mediation does not work out, you have to go to trial. Keep in mind that you are the one on trial, so you tell your lawyer what you want to do. When you are with this lawyer, you can ask as many questions as you want. Definitely ask questions, if things don't feel right to you. This lawyer must give you anything the court has given them. Make sure you have copies of every piece of paper and understand everything about what is going on in court. There are even cd's you can get of the recordings in the trial. Listening to the cd's can help you better prepare for the next session. Again, you are the one on trial, so use everything you can to win. If you feel you are being misrepresented or your lawyer is not doing a good job, fire them. But understand you're going to have to start over again if you go with a different firm.

Going to court and hiring lawyers is going to cost you money. This is why it is best to try to work things out, but sometimes that is not possible. Lawyers may charge you anything from $150 - $400 an hour. Some law firms will have you pay a retainer anywhere from $5,000 - $10,000. This is a lot of money. This is also the reason some people choose to represent themselves in court and others give up.

The thought of going to court, doing all this preparation, spending thousands of dollars and potentially losing, having to pay more, and not getting anything you asked for is very discouraging and frustrating. The only thing that is worse than this is having your child think you didn't try for them and that you left them in this world without their dad.

MAN TO MAN

For the men out in this world not taking care of their children, wake up and start handling your business! When I say men, I'm referring to a male that is out of school and has a job. It is time you take accountability and responsibility for the child you helped bring in this world. If you don't want the responsibility of taking care of children, don't have any. You can use a condom, or you can go to a doctor and have a procedure done called a vasectomy, this will stop you from having children. I wouldn't recommend doing this at a young age unless you are absolutely sure you don't ever want to have children. If you have a child in this world and you don't make an attempt to do anything for that child, you are not a real man and you deserve no respect.

Being in a child's life, watching them grow and become a person, is such a beautiful thing to witness, as long as they are on the right path. Whether they stay on the right path falls in the hands of TWO (2) determined parents. Do you have to sacrifice some time? Yes. Is it going to cost you some money? Yes. These thoughts should have been the determining factor before you laid down with that woman. You should have a job (preferably one with health benefits) before you lay down with any woman in that capacity.

Children really aren't a lot of money, in my experience, and I don't deprive my children of anything. Keep in mind, you have about nine months to save up some money. The most expensive thing in their early lives (assuming you have health insurance and after baby formula) is childcare. But if childcare is needed, that would imply both parents are working. If you are one of those men who sits at home doing nothing productive while your woman goes to work after dropping the baby off at the babysitter, find one of those big dumpsters in an alley and throw yourself in it.

There are great fathers in this world who cannot contribute all that much financially. But what they can contribute is their time. Being there for your child is just as important as supporting them financially. I'm not saying being around your children should substitute financial support but being in their lives and being there for them when they need you is important too. Just a person to talk to or some attention is all your baby needs at the time. Money can provide food, shelter, and some opportunities. But being in your child's life completes the bigger part of the puzzle. Morals and value development and character building should happen in the house at a young age. It's better for your child to have a role model in the house instead of the drug dealer at the corner. Especially if you have a son, a boy looks to his father for guidance until he loses confidence in his dad.

The next most expensive thing associated with children is money for college. This is the big one, this can cost you anywhere from $150,000 - $250,000. I know it seems like a lot of money and it is, but this can be achieved. When your child is a baby start saving for college right away. There are financial consultants that can sit down with you and help you come up with a plan to save. Instead of spending all the tax money on things you don't need, save some of it and put in the college fund. There are stocks and other money building steps you can do also. Saving money for college is not impossible.

In my experience, these are the two biggest financial issues associated with raising children. This, again, is assuming you have health insurance, and you don't face any serious medical problems down the road. Buying children food and clothing, which you have to do pretty often, really isn't all that expensive if you are smart about purchases. Children do not need name brand clothes and the newest sneakers.

If you are one of those men who does nothing for your kid, get it together and do your part now. If you are unemployed, get a job. If you have a substance abuse problem or anger management issues, get the help you need. This world is rough, and these children out here need their dad, they need us. Are you going to stand up, man up, and handle it? If not get snipped, sit down, and get out of the real man's way. You are making us look bad.

FINAL WORD

William, I pray these words find you healthy and happy and in a place where you understand that I love you and I haven't abandoned you. As I have stated before, my primary reason for writing this book was to reach out to you. I also wrote this book to help myself and help other people, if they share this problem. I got through many tough days by writing this book, imagining I was talking to you. It is still extremely painful and frustrating knowing you are in this world and I can't be with you.

Thank God for our family, in particular my wife, who has been the one listening to my whining, rubbing my back, and telling me everything is going to be alright. She has always had my back, been extremely supportive in everything I've ever done, and she is always very encouraging. She is an amazing woman and makes me exceedingly happy. I pray that you find someone with her qualities. Your brother keeps me distracted being his charming self. When I interact with him, I imagine you two are alike and it makes me smile, thinking I'm with you too. Your grandmother also lets me vent and is just as hurt as I am. She wrote you something:

For My Darling William

Dear Peanut, (My nickname for you when you were inside your mother's belly!)

I used to talk to you, awaiting your arrival. I was so excited, I couldn't wait to meet the unique little person who would be my grandson. I am still waiting to meet you in person and will never give up hope that I will see you soon. Until then, there are some things I will share with you. I love you and pray for your happiness and well-being everyday. You are a member of a large and loving family, they are praying for you also. I know my savior, Jesus Christ is watching over you in my place. Please know it is our wish for you to learn to have real love, kindness, honesty, and strong faith. Even though you can't be with me to learn the things I share with your brother and sister, I will find a way to pass it on to you. Most importantly, you are so loved, even though you don't know us. Be strong and of good courage. Do good and anything evil will not be able to dwell where you are.

Love Always,

Grandma Blythe

If I sold 10 million books, and you weren't one of the readers, I did not complete my primary objective. Though if I could in some way help that many people, encourage someone to write to their absent child, or convince someone to step up and be a parent; I would be very happy with that. Things don't always happen how we intend them to, but I guess it was God's intentions for it to happen the way it happened.

To my brothers out there who have their hearts in the right place, if you have attempted to be in your child's life so you can be with them and take care of them, you are not a deadbeat! If a man is not in his child's life, the world assumes it is the man that doesn't want to be around. People need to understand that is not always the case. If you have a story similar to mine, don't give up the fight. I realize, no matter what you do, you are always looked at as the problem or looked at as if you're not doing enough. But don't let that discourage you, keep fighting for your baby, you do have rights. My goal here is to open your eyes and let you know there is something you can do. I know you are frustrated and brokenhearted like I am, but I implore you to keep going. You can write a book telling your side of the story, it definitely helped me. Or do something else that will help you reach out to your baby and help you deal with all the pain.

To my brothers out there not doing anything for your children, even when asked for help, start helping. It's that simple.

Finally, William this book (which took me about a year to write) would probably be a 3-day conversation. I have a lifetime of things to tell you. I have a lifetime of memories to share with you. I can't get to you right now, but I will not stop trying. However, the reality is that you might have to find me one day. I will be here, and I will be waiting for you.

P.S. You are going to be a big brother!

Made in the USA
Middletown, DE
28 April 2021